MORE TV VICAR?

MORE TV VICAR?

Christians on the Telly:
The Good, the Bad and the Quirky

BRYONY TAYLOR

DARTON·LONGMAN+TODD

First published in 2015 by
Darton, Longman and Todd Ltd
1 Spencer Court
140–142 Wandsworth High Street
London SW18 4JJ

ISBN 978-0-232-53170-1

All biblical quotations are taken from the NRSV

A catalogue record for this book is available from the British Library.

Designed and typeset by Judy Linard
Printed and bound by ScandBook AB, Sweden

**For Paul,
my husband and best friend**

Contents

Acknowledgements

There are a number of people to thank without whom this book would not be in your hands now. First, thank you to Paul, my husband, who has been a constant encourager as I have been writing and incredibly gracious, and also came up with the book title. Thanks and lots of love to my fantastic family, the Halls and the Taylors – my cheerleaders. Thank you to Revd Dr Michael Volland, my college tutor, who gave me advice and support as I started this book and to Revd Canon Sue Pinnington MBE, my training incumbent who took me on with this book part-written!

Thanks to those who contributed to the book: James Cary and Paul Kerensa who provided much food for thought and expertise; Revd Dr Kate Bruce and Revd Alice Snowden for the great conversations about comedy and faith. Thanks to my friends at Cranmer Hall who let me read extracts of the book to them and gave me generous feedback. Thanks to Dr Bex Lewis, a constant friend and fellow writer and to Frankie Edwards for the advice on writing and publishing. Thank you to the brothers of Alnmouth Friary for their kind hospitality in the Summer of 2014 where I had space to write.

A big thank you to my friends and collaborators online, Revd Robb Sutherland and Nick Morgan, who have taught me about satire and its uses and abuses and been all round good disciples of Christ and companions on the journey.

Lastly, thank you to you for reading. I hope this book helps you to know 'life in all its fullness' (John 10:10) a little more.

Deo Gratias.

January 2015

Preface

'When I was young, all TV vicars were wet, soppy figures, played by people like Dick Emery and Derek Nimmo.'
— Diederick Santer, producer of *Grantchester*[1]

I admit it, I am a telly addict. I just completed one of those quizzes on Facebook and scored 19/20 on 1980s television adverts. I watch a lot of telly. I am also interested in culture and I do think in recent years television has begun to be recognised as an art form in its own right – let's face it, many of us are more excited about the latest HBO TV release than the latest films on at the cinema. What we see on television provides us with a mirror to our society. The types of programmes that get airtime present something of the prevailing values of our culture. We also, although I wouldn't like to admit it, are heavily influenced by what we watch on television. If I see something on BBC Four I think it must be gospel. It's BBC Four after all – that's like the Oxbridge of television channels. If I see something on ITV2 I take it with a pinch of salt, but it still influences me (mainly to do my shopping at Iceland – but that's a kind of influence too, it just won't help me in a pub quiz).

I also admit that I'm a Christian (hey, that's not so easy

in this day and age. It's like saying you're a trainspotter but worse). Actually, recently, I've done more than that – I've become part of the strange arcane world of the clergy. I wear a bit of white plastic around my collar and I can put 'Revd' in front of my name.

I've noticed that adults' attitudes to ministers of religion do not grow up as their views of other professions do. When you are a child you think all teachers live in the school and are mortified when you see them buying Andrex at the supermarket. Adults feel this way about vicars. Surely vicars don't have normal lives? I've had all sorts of people ask odd questions such as, 'Are you allowed to get married?' (bit late if I'm not!), or people tut when I pick up a chocolate éclair from a buffet as if that's somehow out of bounds to a 'woman of the cloth' (a lovely archaic phrase that people like to use for weird folk like me). The wonderful Revd Kate Bottley has recently started a one woman crusade against this prevailing view of the clergy by appearing regularly on *Gogglebox* on Channel 4 – a programme much more fun than it sounds. It shows different groups of people watching a selection of television programmes that you probably watched yourself the week before, and making witty or inane comments. In it, Revd Kate sits sipping tea and commenting on television in much the same way as the other families featured on the programme. Keep up the good work Kate!

But where do these prevailing views of Christians as freaks, geeks or antiques[2] come from? It's likely that a lot of them come from the television itself. I thought it would be fun to have a look at some portrayals of Christians on British television and see what they have to say about this. Some you will know really well, some

Preface

you might not have heard of, but this book constitutes a tour of a wild array of the good, the bad and the quirky. I hope to shed some light on these characters, why they are portrayed as they are, and what that says about society's view of Christians – and how weird Christians like me should respond to them.

Introduction

**'If you are religious, that's OK,
but you've got to keep analysing it,
and keep a sense of humour, because
without a sense of humour people
start dying.'**
— Eddie Izzard[1]

If I asked you to describe a 'typical Christian' to me, what would you say? What sort of characteristics come first to your mind? What is your typical Christian wearing? What kind of music do they like? Or are you struggling to even picture what a Christian might be like at all?

The chances are that the first mental images that came to your mind have been informed by popular culture – and particularly by the diet that you have been fed through the television over the years. In this book, I explore the menu on offer on British television screens of various 'Christian' characters. What does this say about our culture? How do you react to these characters? Are they truthful or pure invention?

There are all kinds of reactions we might have to different characters on screen. Often these are related to our own sense of identity and identification with the type being presented. Sometimes the bias of the television or film makers is completely hidden to us – depending on the position we are coming from. This is illustrated neatly by the Bechdel test, named after American cartoonist Alison Bechdel. This is a test that can be applied to any work of fiction to identify if there is a gender bias. To pass the test the work must contain two named female characters who talk to each other about something other than a man.[2] If you evaluate films in this way you will quickly discover the hidden gender bias in much of the output of Hollywood.

Perhaps there is a hidden bias at play on our televisions when it comes to portraying Christian characters? The BBC has certainly been accused of being anti-Christian in recent years.[3] This is becoming an increasingly delicate subject with the reality of persecution of Christians around the world and the rise of extremist groups like ISIS responding violently to critiques of Islam. Free speech is back on the agenda and characters with religious connections on our TV increasingly have the potential to cause offence. I don't think I could create a test as neat as Alison Bechdel's but what I am hoping to do here is provide a lens through which we might interpret what we see on our televisions – and have some fun in the process.

Being a Christian and also being a big fan of television, I wanted to explore how and why Christians are portrayed on British television – is there a shift happening and is this reflecting something of where we are as a society? To do this I have split the characters I found into three categories: the good, the bad and the quirky. To some extent, these are crude categories but I hope they provide a helpful framework through which to explore the uniqueness of British culture, the nature of satire and offence and our ongoing fascination with people who are 'other'.

The first category is the 'good'. This category contains those wholesome loveable characters who don't seem to have a bad bone in their body. I explore the connections between nostalgia and the countryside and how this seems often to include the church – especially the Church of England. I then look at some more recent characters we have seen that are 'warts and all', i.e. more related to reality, more fully rounded figures who we can imagine meeting in our real lives. I explore why newer Christian characters on the television are becoming more fully rounded and believable. I consider why there is still an attraction for television writers in creating Christian characters when at the same time the story in the press is that the church is in terminal decline.

The second category is the 'bad'. In this category I look at some characters who are the diametric opposite to their assumed role – such as the Baby-Eating Bishop of Bath and Wells from *Blackadder* – those characters who are made wholly evil for a brilliant joke. In addition to this stand-up comedy is now a big feature of the television schedules so I couldn't avoid in this section the rise of the atheist comedian in Britain and the growing hostility to religious belief on the comedy circuit. Is this changing people's perception of people of faith? What about the nature of offence and satire? How far is too far? These are topics very pertinent at present with the debates around free speech and recent terrorist attacks on satirists in France and Denmark.

Lastly I will look at those characters who do not fit neatly into the good or bad category – those who are simply quirky. These are characters who are identifiably Christian but are eccentric – such as Father Ted, the long-suffering priest from Craggy Island. I also take a tour of the many clerical characters played by Rowan Atkinson over the years and look at what they say about changing attitudes to Christians and the church.

To conclude I make some suggestions as to where we go from here. What would Jesus think of these characters? What are the origins of our famed sense of humour in Britain and what does the church have to do with them?

It is all about context. Gentle teasing is a sign of affection in British culture but can be misconstrued. I learnt this the hard way when I lived abroad for some time and had a Finnish roommate. We were in a shop and she asked the woman behind the counter for four doughnuts. The woman replied, 'Four?' in a rather surprised manner. I nudged my friend and said, 'Ooh, you pig!' As we left the shop (with my friend clutching her four doughnuts in a bag) she turned to me, face downcast and said, 'Do you really think I am a pig?' I replied nonchalantly and said, 'Of course not, I was only joking!' and she said 'But it's not funny.' That was me told: I felt terrible!

It is so easy for us to misinterpret each other and misinterpret people's intentions. In this book I want to get under the skin of some of television's best loved 'Christian' characters to see exactly what is going on. What are the creators of these characters trying to say and do, and what does our response say about us? Perhaps, sometimes, things are lost in translation. What follows might serve as a bit of a Rough Guide. We'll stop off at the popular sites and then meander down some less well travelled paths to get a sense of the landscape of British culture and attitudes to Christianity and hopefully we'll be able to come back from our trip, like all good pilgrimages, having had a great time, a little bit more worldly wise and refreshed in our outlook on life.

MORE TV VICAR?

The 'good'

**'I thought, "How on earth do you play
a central character who's so blooming good?" I
thought, "Where are the flaws? Where is
the monster in this woman?" That's what
I understand comedy to be.'**[1]
— Dawn French on playing the Vicar of Dibley

Old England

Imagine an English country village: you see a duck pond with a child fishing for sticklebacks with a small net, a post office with a cheery lady wearing a floral tabard sorting brown paper packages tied up with string, a cosy pub with an old farmer smoking a pipe propping up the bar talking about the price of pig feed, an idyllic church with a creaky old lychgate and tooth-like wonky gravestones scattered in a churchyard, a stray sheep here and there in the middle of the road and to top off the scene a vicar on a bike winding his way down the main street wearing a cassock blowing in the wind as he goes to visit old Mrs Whittaker for a cup of tea and a slice of cake.

This is completely recognisable. It's true and not true: a mixture of personal experience, nostalgia and history. No surprise, then, that people can have a view of the church as a relic of the past – generally a benign one – but still a relic. We can recognise quite readily the description of the narrator's 'boring village' in Dodie Smith's *I Capture the Castle*:

> 'The village is tiny: just the church, the vicarage, the little school, the inn, one shop (which is also the post office) and a huddle of cottages; though the Vicar gets quite a congregation from the surrounding hamlets and farms.'

Although written in 1948, this could well have been written now (maybe with the exception of 'quite a congregation'!) The image of the idyllic country village is simply not complete without the church and its vicar. Even with post offices closing and pubs being shut down, the churches remain.

Because of this we often find a strong connection between media portrayals of 'good' Christian characters and nostalgia. Many of the cosy and cuddly Christian characters from popular culture are seen in the context of the countryside – something about which people have been nostalgic since time immemorial (from the Greek poet Hesiod, through to Virgil and later Shakespeare and Dickens).

Old England, a place that has never existed in reality, exists rather powerfully in the popular imagination. I get puffed up when I hear or read Shakespeare's description from *Richard II*:

> 'This royal throne of kings, this sceptred isle,
> This earth of majesty, this seat of Mars,
> This other Eden, demi-paradise...'

'This other Eden, demi-paradise...' Really? The country of Tupperware-coloured[2] grey skies and queues in the rain, where, to quote the band Blur, 'all the high streets look the same'?[3] No one in their right mind would ever describe our country as a demi-paradise (even in Shakespeare's day) but curiously we want to believe it and hearing England described as such gives us a warm fuzzy feeling – even though we know it to be completely inaccurate!

Memory and nostalgia play tricks on us – or rather, perhaps, we use memory and nostalgia to deal with an unpleasant reality. Elizabeth Loftus, Professor of Psychology and Social Behaviour at the University of California, has researched memory and shown that false memories can even be implanted in the brain.[4] The desire to believe something as true in the face of an otherwise bleak reality is very strong. Loftus explains:

'Our memories have a superiority complex. We remember we got better grades than we did, that we voted in elections we didn't vote in, that we gave more money to charity than we did, that our kids walked and talked earlier than they really did. It's not that we're lying. It's just something that happens naturally to allow us to feel a little better about ourselves.'[5]

Couple this natural deceit of the brain with nostalgia and you have a potent cocktail.

Research into nostalgia has shown that it can be 'good for us' in that it can counteract loneliness and anxiety. An experiment at Southampton University showed that on cold days or in cold rooms people are able to use nostalgic thoughts to make themselves literally feel warm.[6] This is all at play when considering scenes of Old England – particularly country scenes. Comedians Mitchell and Webb illustrate this in a hilarious spoof advertisement for 'The ultimate Sunday afternoon chill out DVD':

> 'Toast the crumpet of your soul on these images, let out a puddingy burp and enjoy... Over the next 14 hours we will be lulling you into sofa-ry oblivion, with, among other things, all the establishing shots of ITV's *Kingdom* (but without anything as jolting as the plot), vicars walking across lawns, some pretty objects from the *Antiques Roadshow*...a crossword being filled in with the names of characters from *Dad's Army* and then smeared with delicious jam...'[7]

The cosy images being conjured up for this 'relaxation DVD' include vicars walking across lawns! It's funny and a bit preposterous but this highlights how much the church and vicars are a part of this rural fantasy. There's something heart-warming about the idea of a vicar sitting by a fireside discussing family news in a genial manner over a glass of sherry. It fits the fantasy.

I spent two weeks one summer learning about the challenges of rural ministry. Although I can remember that some of the things faced by the church in the countryside are very difficult, such as low employment, decrepit buildings, bad harvests and bat infestations, my overwhelming memory of the fortnight is the amount of tea and cake I consumed. I know that this is not the main thing I should be remembering but my brain is deceitful, it's made a shortcut and decided that rural ministry = tea and cake, despite the evidence to the contrary in black and white in my journal. What is it about the countryside that does this to us?

The past is usually viewed through rose tinted spectacles and because Christians, traditionally, are supposed to be 'good' they become part of this fantasy. 'In the old days, everyone was lovely, you could leave your house unlocked and people had time for each other' people might say. The bumbling, friendly vicar character encapsulates this idyll and becomes a symbol of 'all things wholesome'. This stereotype of the lovely friendly vicar (whose only vice is a love of chocolate or a tipple of sherry every now and then) often only works when placed in the past or in a world alien to a lot of people's experience – such as the countryside. Put that soft bumbling vicar character into inner city Leeds, calling in at the kebab shop, trying to reason with drug addicts, dealing with the issue of stolen lead from the church roof and handing out food parcels at the food bank and it just doesn't work. It has to be outside of everyday experience – ordinary life with all its challenges and problems simply bursts the bubble of the nostalgic reverie.

Portrayals of Christians who are inherently 'good' in nature have to be put into the context of nostalgic fantasy for people to believe in them – then they will believe in them with gusto, even in the face of what we know to be the truth (that no one is really that wholesome). The 'goodness' of the character has to be their defining characteristic. When the character is fairly one-dimensional in this way they are almost always placed in a historical or nostalgic setting.

These 'good' Christian characters in this bucolic and nostalgic setting are also often from the Church of England: to work, they almost *need* to be. One could argue that this is because most of the churches in the countryside are

Church of England, or that it is the established Church and so is to be expected. I think, however, that it is more likely that, because of its reputation for 'woolliness', it fits this hazy nostalgic world. Kate Fox, writing of the English's attitude to religion says:

> 'the Church of England is the least religious church on earth. It is notoriously woolly-minded, tolerant to a fault and amiably non-prescriptive.'

Nowhere is this better illustrated than in a classic sketch by comedian Eddie Izzard, comparing the 'good old C of E' with the Spanish Inquisition. Eddie points out that the C of E would have been useless at running the Spanish Inquisition because they would give a person being tortured on the rack a choice of 'tea and cake or death?' and, inevitably, the victim would say 'cake, please!'[8]

Because of its reputation of being non-prescriptive, the Church of England is very malleable. It can easily slot into a rural image because it's squishy enough to do so. Try it with the Scottish Presbyterian Church or the Roman Catholic Church and you struggle – they're too rigid and spiky. Imagine an Anglican vicar in a country church and you can already guess what it would be like to shake his hand at the end of the service: clammy and nervous, like an awkward teenager on a date trying not to appear too keen as he asks you if you want to stay for a cup of tea. I just made that up, but you believe it don't you?

Perhaps because the Church of England is 'ours' (as in established) – and what Kate Fox calls our 'default' religion,[9] we find it easier to tease and make fun of it. Just as we might reserve our harshest caricature for our closest family members we treat the C of E as an eccentric old aunt, loveable but fair game for a bit of teasing. Indeed, George Carey, on becoming Archbishop of Canterbury in 1991 described the Church of England in just such a way:

> 'I see it as an elderly lady who mutters away to herself in the corner, ignored most of the time.'[10]

It is astonishing that its own leader would describe it like this but it shows the strength of this image of the C of E as part of the family of the English, one of our own that we can commandeer to take part in any escapist story we like.

So go and make yourself a nice cup of tea with gold top milk, take a biscuit out of a biscuit tin with a country scene depicted on it, or a piece of homemade cake bought at a church fete for 5p, make yourself comfortable on a wicker chair in your conservatory, have a look at a reproduction of Constable's *The Hay Wain*, hum the opening strains of *The Archers*' theme tune and come on a tour with me of a couple of the best 'good' Christian characters.

 # FATHER BROWN

Category: Good ☑ Bad ☐ Quirky ☐
Name: Father Brown
Actor: Mark Williams

Character details

Father Brown is a creation of writer G.K. Chesterton who published five compilations of stories from 1911–36. Father Brown is a scruffy, clever, Roman Catholic priest dedicated to solving mysteries with an insight into the human propensity for evil. He is perhaps a strong contrast with that other great fictional detective, Sherlock Holmes, as he uses spiritual and philosophical reasoning to reach his conclusions. Chesterton's stories about Father Brown have provided rich fodder for television producers; most recently (2013) in a BBC series starring Mark Williams as Father Brown.

Score card:

Longevity	92%
Endearment	95%
Offence	8%
Vices	23%
Popularity	75%
Realism	41%

Father Brown

'Has it never struck you that a man who does next to nothing but hear men's real sins is not likely to be wholly unaware of human evil?'

— G.K. Chesterton, *The Blue Cross*

In 2013, the BBC ran a new daytime television series based on the Father Brown detective stories of G.K. Chesterton. Knowing that Father Brown had successfully been brought to the screen before (and that a gentle crime series works well on daytime television) the producers decided to bring him back with Mark Williams in the lead role. Intriguingly, the original stories are set in London in the Edwardian and inter-war periods, but the producers this time decided to set the whole series in the Cotswolds – that 'biscuit tin perfect' part of the English countryside *and* move the period to a nostalgic (i.e. within living memory) 1950s. Part of this decision was to help 'sell' England abroad but also the 'city' does not represent comfort or cosiness to people wanting to escape: cities, by their nature are brash, new and fast changing. Many people watching daytime television would be able to remember the 1950s – further adding to the nostalgia effect. Add a friendly, quirky, clergy character to the mix and you're guaranteed a hit. The 'vicar' character 'fits'.

Curiously, the vicar character whom we see portrayed in nostalgic countryside scenes in people's minds is exactly that – a vicar, not a Catholic priest, a member of that woolly, friendly, undemanding denomination, the Church of England. Having moved him from his London setting, Father Brown, the Roman Catholic priest, comes across more as a Church of England vicar in its Cotswolds setting – a setting in which it would be unlikely to find an ancient and picturesque country church that was Roman Catholic. Here, perhaps, recent scandals that have hit the Roman Catholic Church and particularly the reputation of its clergy are muted by the new rural and chintzy 1950s setting – so much so that you almost forget he's Roman Catholic at all.

The success of this character is also down to the fact that he has become a 'classic' – the Father Brown stories are among the best loved of G.K. Chesterton's work and were published long ago enough not to be tainted by modern current affairs. Brown is literally the Father of sleuthing clergy characters – just as Sherlock Holmes is the father of literary detectives. Chesterton was on to something when he observed that a priest would hear many confessions and would make a great detective figure, as he says through Father Brown:

> 'Has it never struck you that a man who does next to nothing but hear men's real sins is not likely to be wholly unaware of human evil?'
>
> — G.K. Chesterton, *The Blue Cross*

The 'good'

There is a great contrast between the 'good' priest and the 'evil' criminals he helps to catch. Having said this, the character of Father Brown is not wholly one dimensional (as some of these country vicars characters can be). Speaking of reproducing *The Blue Cross* for the BBC, Mark Williams points out:

> 'In the original story, there's a moment where Father Brown throws some soup up a wall as he leaves a restaurant…Those are the kinds of moments that I like where he does something very shocking in terms of social behaviour. We tried to get a few of those in there.'[11]

If I were writing this book in the early years of the last century, it is likely that this character would be pushed into the 'accurate' portrayals section in the next chapter. Chesterton did indeed base Father Brown on a real priest, Father John O'Connor (1870–1952), who had had a particular influence on his conversion to Catholicism. Chesterton was able to share some of his own views of faith and belief through the character of Father Brown. It is significant, I think, that this particular portrayal has come from a Christian writer. It has an air of authenticity (even given the daytime television treatment) that is missing in some of the other Christian characters we see.

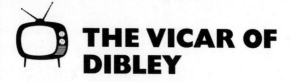 # THE VICAR OF DIBLEY

Category: Good ☑ Bad ☐ Quirky ☐
Name: Geraldine Granger, the Vicar of Dibley
Actor: Dawn French

Programme details

Created by Richard Curtis for the BBC, this popular sitcom ran from 1994–2007. When an old vicar dies in the small, conservative country parish of Dibley the parish are sent a replacement in the form of lively vicar, Geraldine Granger – the shock factor not being that she loves rock music and chocolate but that she is a woman. This is a classic sitcom format with regular clashes between the innovator Geraldine and the eccentric villagers led by reactionary churchwarden David Horton (Gary Waldhorn). Each episode ends with Geraldine telling a (usually inappropriate) joke to slow-witted Alice Tinker (Emma Chambers), the verger.

Score card:

Longevity	89%
Endearment	92%
Offence	21%
Vices	65%
Popularity	99%
Realism	42%

The Vicar of Dibley

'You were expecting a bloke – beard, bible, bad breath…
And instead you got a babe with a bob cut and a magnificent
bosom.'

— Geraldine Granger, *The Vicar of Dibley*,
Series 1, Episode 1

The Vicar of Dibley is the queen of all these nostalgic portrayals of 'good' Christians.

For most people (clergy often excepted) the thought of Dawn French as the Vicar of Dibley raises a smile – it conjures up an image of a rural idyll, a bygone era, a time when life was more innocent. The Revd Geraldine Granger first burst onto our television screens in 1994. Richard Curtis, the writer, realised the comedic potential of putting a radical and, most importantly, female vicar character into a sleepy conservative country parish shortly after the vote to allow the ordination of women to the priesthood in the Church of England.

The comedy in the sitcom is based around the clash of cultures – town versus country, progressive versus reactionary and, of course, male versus female. For the comedy to work, these cultures needed to be extremes. The Parish of Dibley is a figment of our imagination: a country parish complete with country bumpkins, gruff farmers and a never-ending parish council meeting. The rural setting of Dibley is a place that has never existed in reality – it was a fantasy world from the outset, engineered to press all the right buttons to generate that warm fuzzy feeling: it is even evident in the filter used on the camera to make the countryside scenes glow with light. Richard Curtis shared why he chose this setting in a documentary about the programme:

> 'village life...is much sweeter and much gentler and more understanding and tolerant than city life is, so I actually think it's one of the dreams of England that's still actually got a bit of truth in it.'[12]

In the same documentary the actor James Fleet, who plays Hugo, goes on to say: 'It's not 'modern Britain' at all is it? It's some weird kind of fantasy world.'

The biggest joke in *The Vicar of Dibley* is that the new vicar is a woman. Twenty years on, this shock factor is no longer there. Yet at the time it was created there was still quite a lot of opposition to the idea of a woman priest. This 'fantasy world' was used almost as a Trojan horse to help change attitudes to women's ministry in Britain and beyond:

> 'It did have a campaigning feeling at the beginning, I actually seriously wanted people by the end of the series to think, "This is completely right."'
>
> — Richard Curtis[13]

It is hard to imagine how people's attitudes would be if it hadn't been for this wildly popular sitcom that appealed to the very people (Middle England) who might have been opposed to women's ministry. Richard Curtis put words into the characters' mouths that he had heard at the General Synod of the Church of England as they debated women's ordination:

'If Jesus had wanted women to spread the gospel he would have appointed them. It's Matthew, Mark, Luke and John, not Sharon, Tracy, Tara and Debbie!'
— David Horton, *The Vicar of Dibley*,
Series 1, Episode 1

As the series progressed so did people's views: to a certain extent it changed the image of the Church of England as well. Up to this point the only portrayals of clergy on television had been of bumbling incompetents, arch hypocrites or camp curates. The familiar image of a Church of England minister would be a character played by Derek Nimmo with his plummy voice, such as the Revd Mervyn Noote in the 1960s clerical sitcom *All Gas and Gaiters* (a comedy about a Bishop who hates the Dean with whom he has to work). Suddenly we were shown that church didn't have to be like that. People joke about the episode of *The Vicar of Dibley* with the 'pet' service but many rural vicars have started similar innovations – a quick Google search will find you all manner of resources for hosting your own pet service in church.

I spoke to the Revd Alice Snowden who was at theological college as the series was first aired: 'She was the first TV cleric that we'd laughed *with* rather than at.' Alice suggests that the series gave the laity a language for talking about what seemed right or wrong about having a woman priest – it was a good way into conversations, 'I don't know if you've seen this programme...' The genuine vocation of women priests was well expressed by the first episode, as Alice told me:

> 'The episode when Geraldine preaches about how she'd planned to be a fashion model but was blown away by the Sermon on the Mount instead is genuinely moving and inspiring – not only that she'd had that depth of spiritual experience but that she became a priest because of this sense of calling, not out of any sense of wanting to do it just because she could – many people did think that women offered themselves for the priesthood just to make a feminist point.'

Some of the objections to Geraldine Granger in the programme seem ludicrous to us now but as Revd Alice points out they represent some women priests' real experience of meeting people who couldn't quite put their finger on it but just 'knew' that it wasn't a suitable job for a woman. What *The Vicar of Dibley* did was expose some of these views for what they were and shift people's perceptions of having a woman in the role of priest.

The only place left for *The Vicar of Dibley* to go has been to explore the consecration of women as bishops – and Richard Curtis manages to get a little dig in at the Church of England in the recent special episode created for Comic Relief 2015. Geraldine is invited to go for interview for a post of bishop and finds herself competing with a group of five others. When challenged by another candidate to tell a joke (because she's famously hilarious), Geraldine fails but then says:

> 'The whole point is that this situation is what's funny, that's the joke, because if we were all men, we'd be bishops by now wouldn't we?'[14]

Touché!

I think the series has done its job. It can now be watched on Comedy Gold-type channels but is no longer aired on mainstream channels. The idea of a woman priest is no longer a big joke. To use the shock factor for humour, writers have had to look for other settings – such as the army (see 2013 sitcom *Bluestone 42*) in which to depict a woman priest.

The Vicar of Dibley, then, is unique in both having created a fantasy world that makes people feel warm and fuzzy *and* in challenging people to imagine doing church differently.

Think 'woman priest' and you immediately think of the Vicar of Dibley, there won't be a woman priest in the country who hasn't at some time or other been compared to her. Although she's not *universally* loved as a character, it could have been a lot worse – the enduring image of a 'woman priest' in the popular imagination is fun, irreverent, 'normal' and cares about people:

> 'So here I am, at your service, totally yours, any time, any day. Although if you come to see me first thing in the morning, wear dark glasses, because before my face falls into place I look frighteningly like Bernard Manning.'
> — Revd Geraldine Granger, *The Vicar of Dibley*,
> Series 1, Episode 1

What is going on here?

The most obvious 'hidden question' behind these rural Christian stereotypes was summed up by Dawn French as she describes Geraldine Granger's character as 'so blooming good' – are Christians really that good? There is a hidden assumption that to be a Christian and especially to be a member of the clergy, that you have to be good. The defining characteristic of a Christian in this mould is 'a nice person' – a British person might typically say 'almost too nice'. We are naturally distrustful of people who come across as good and wholesome.

The problem with coming across as 'good' is that it can work as code for 'boring'. George Whitefield observed this when he famously said, 'Why should the devil have all the best tunes?'[15]

This simple kind of dualism is often at play when people

consider a Christian character – they are either squeaky clean or morally repugnant – there are no shades of grey when it comes to caricature.

Any 'good' Christian character that 'works' for people now has to be put in the setting of the fantasy of Old England, and if possible, the countryside. There is a hint here that people believe that that kind of character simply no longer exists. The funny thing is that it never existed in the first place. Dawn French when she was asked to play a vicar came with an assumption that you can't be funny and good at the same time. She discovered that this wasn't true when she visited the (real) Revd Joy Carroll's house with Richard Curtis and saw that she had a mug that said 'Lead me not into temptation, I can find it myself.'[16] Seeing this gave him permission to write a character who had quirks and flaws, as well as happening to be a member of the Anglican clergy.

According to anthropologist, Kate Fox, English people hate earnestness; we have a deep suspicion of anyone who comes across as too earnest or good:

> 'Seriousness is acceptable, solemnity is prohibited. Sincerity is allowed, earnestness is strictly forbidden. Pomposity and self-importance are outlawed. Serious matters can be spoken of seriously, but one must never take *oneself* too seriously.'[17]

Here we can see the root of Dawn French's initial reluctance to play a vicar character. Interestingly, however, the stereotype of the priest being someone 'other', 'not like us' is still very powerful. Almost all clergy have to spend time trying to say 'I'm just like you'. There is something about the dog collar that creates this fake persona that has never existed – that is, to quote Mary Poppins, 'practically perfect in every way'. I have a priest friend who has piercings, tattoos and long hair, plays in a metal band and drives a Harley Davidson. Every time he moves to a new parish he makes the local newspaper by sheer dint of being himself. It is still shocking that a vicar might have ordinary interests or even be 'normal'. Derek Nimmo has a lot to answer for!

Our response

How do you respond to these cosy, countryside portrayals of Christians? Do they make you wistful? Irritated? Angry?

Is a bit of nostalgia essentially harmless or is it a dangerous fantasy to have?

We shouldn't ignore the affection with which these characters are drawn. It is refreshing to have Christian characters who are well loved rather than roundly criticised or that are a direct critique of the church in the media. Although some of these characters can be one dimensional, they are still positive depictions of Christians in an increasingly hostile world.

The danger, however, is two-fold – the first is in perpetuating the idea of the vicar or Christian 'practically perfect in every way', which reinforces the 'not like us' view. This brings into even sharper relief the shock which is felt when the church is beset with catastrophic scandals. The second is in cynically believing that people can never be wholesome or good or have purely good intentions at heart – which can be equally damaging – people then look for scandal when it isn't there.

I think it is important to recognise both the fantasy

and the reality in these portrayals – part of it is there to reassure and comfort and the other to remind us that good is possible: it's worth spending time dwelling on that.

Priests are people too

A new trend in current portrayals of Christians in the media is that of gritty realism. Gone are the stereotypes of old – the bumbling, friendly, country parson and the two-dimensional figures who act as useful plot devices; in are well-rounded depictions of flawed individuals. The bubble of Christendom has burst. We are now in an age where the church contends with scandal on a daily basis. No longer is it possible, or believable, to have 'whiter than white' depictions of Christians in the media – those, if they do still exist, are relegated to history (such as in 1950s drama *Call the Midwife*[18]) or to the countryside (as I have discussed). Despite there being a fair share of villains who happen to be Christian on television and radio there is also a new breed of 'good' but realistic Christian characters – characters that Christians themselves can identify with.

 # REVD PAUL COATES

Category: Good ☑ Bad ☐ Quirky ☐
Name: Revd Paul Coates
Actor: Arthur Darvill

Character details

Broadchurch is an ITV1 crime drama that first aired in 2013. The Revd Paul Coates is a member of the small community where the murder of a young boy has taken place. In series one he becomes a key person in the life of the village coming to terms with the atrocity but also attracts attention as a potential suspect because of his murky past.

Score card:

Longevity	15%
Endearment	72%
Offence	58%
Vices	63%
Popularity	78%
Realism	82%

The 'good'

Revd Paul Coates – *Broadchurch*

'We are hunted down but never abandoned by God.'

The first of these 'rounded' characters for us to look at is one not from the world of comedy but from drama. *Broadchurch* was a critically acclaimed crime drama first screened on ITV in 2013 with a follow up second series in 2015 and starring David Tennant, Olivia Colman and, playing a young curate, Arthur Darvill (previously known for playing Rory in *Doctor Who*). The series was produced by the same Danish producers of the popular 'Nordic noir' crime thriller *The Killing* and thus reimagined its gritty realism for a British audience and setting.

Part of the intrigue of *Broadchurch* was in the setting – a remote small town by the sea (filmed in Dorset). The storyline of the first series played on the idea of a small town where everyone knows one another, meaning that everyone could be a suspect in the murder case under investigation: in some respects, a classic crime drama set-up but moved into the twenty first century. Of course, we have already seen that if you create an idyllic small town, the church has to be a part of that picture. There is a long pedigree of clergy characters involved in crime storylines – even one of the pieces on a *Cluedo* board is the Reverend Green. So in this classic crime story updated for a modern world they put an 'updated modern curate' character.

Speaking about playing the role, Arthur Darvill, said:

> 'It was my first time playing a man of the cloth, and walking around in a dog collar and robes felt kind of weird. I felt a responsibility when in costume; my language certainly cleaned up a bit.'[19]

Darvill betrays something of the public fascination in the clergy being a 'different breed' in his use of the archaic phrase 'man of the cloth'. There is also an assumption that he mustn't swear (more on that later). That said, the character of Revd Paul Coates is not 'squeaky clean'. Darvill met with a curate as he researched the role:

> 'I went to meet a young vicar before I started filming. He told me that even in the supermarket he is still working,

still a representative of God and the community and as such is always there to help people, to listen. You have a responsibility to live your life in a certain way to keep that respect…you are never not on call.'

This is borne out in the programme in a scene where the curate bumps into the mother of the murdered child in a supermarket car park.

The Revd Paul's character suffers a little from the child abuse scandals that have rocked the church. At one point there is suspicion that because he volunteers at an IT club for boys that he might have inappropriate relationships with them. This, however, rather than an attack on the church is simply portraying the current realities of life as a single male curate. The character also 'has a past' – he has had problems with alcohol. So along with the other key characters in the programme he is relatively 'normal', 'one of us'. This is a departure from the one dimensional vicar characters we have seen before.

What is particularly unusual, and heartening for Christians watching the programme, is the key role given to the Revd Paul of bringing the community together in an act of remembrance and worship at the end of the series. The Revd Paul organises a powerful service in church and then on the beach where he has arranged for beacons to be lit along the coast in memory of the murdered boy. Again, this is simply reflecting real life – in nearly all of the recent great tragedies we have seen on the news, the clergy are the people everyone (including news reporters) turn to. It is one area where the church seems to still have (in the mind of the public) a legitimate part to play.

PADRE MARY GREENSTOCK

Category: Good ☑ Bad ☐ Quirky ☐
Name: Padre Mary Greenstock
Actor: Kelly Adams

Character details

Bluestone 42 is a BBC sitcom created by writers James Cary and Richard Hurst. The programme follows the exploits of a bomb disposal team working in Afghanistan with the added humour that the troop's new chaplain is the attractive Mary who tries to work while rebuffing the constant advances of vain Captain Nick Medhurst.

Score card:

Longevity	18%
Endearment	30%
Offence	61%
Vices	70%
Popularity	25%
Realism	68%

Padre Mary Greenstock – *Bluestone 42*

'Contrary to popular belief, I'm not a nun.'

Bluestone 42 is a controversial BBC Three sitcom featuring a bomb disposal team working in Afghanistan. Much of the humour centres on the fact that the key person who holds the team together back at base, the Padre, is a woman. *Bluestone 42* takes what Richard Curtis did with *The Vicar of Dibley* one step further. One of the few areas where it is still unusual to see a woman priest is in the armed forces. The shock factor that we had nearly twenty years ago with *The Vicar of Dibley* is back in Series 1 and 2 of *Bluestone 42*.

Perhaps another 'shock' factor is that the vicar, played by Kelly Adams, is very attractive. Although this is partly done deliberately to provide plenty of laughs as she automatically becomes the 'love interest' it does reflect another change in attitudes and in the church itself. Recently, London priest Sally Hitchiner was in a magazine feature in *The Times* entitled 'The Vicar wears Prada'. The response from people within and without the church was very strong: people just didn't like the idea that a woman priest might also like to dress well, and might also be attractive: 'Is this really fitting behaviour for a woman of the cloth?' screeched the *Daily Mail*.[20] (That archaic phrase again!)

Because she is nothing like the cosy, friendly, Vicar of Dibley, Padre Mary will never gain a place in the nation's affections in the same way. The Vicar of Dibley set the

mould for the public perception of 'woman priest' – Revd Sally Hitchiner doesn't match it, and neither does Padre Mary.

Having said this, there is still some fascination with the Padre character in the sitcom. She gets grilled by the only other woman in the team (comically surnamed, Bird) about whether she has had sex before or would have sex with any of the men in the team. There remains a fascination with Christians and their sexual morality.

Despite the extreme setting of the sitcom, Mary's character is well-rounded. Like the Revd Paul in *Broadchurch*, she also has a 'past' – this time a problem with gambling. This challenges (helpfully?) the prevailing idea of the priest being 'not one of us'. It also reflects the

The 'good'

reality among the clergy today – more and more people are becoming priests later in life. A higher proportion of the clergy now have had previous careers and in some cases totally different lifestyles from which they have converted to Christianity. We now have an Archbishop of Canterbury who was initially turned away from ordination and who had a career in the oil industry – a far cry from a young man becoming a curate straight out of Oxford at the age of 24.

In Series 2, Mary even finally loses her resolve not to sleep with Captain Nick in an episode that, as writer James Cary warned me it would, had me shouting at the television in dismay! She is all too human in the end – a far cry from the 'too blooming good' Vicar of Dibley. Priests are people too it seems.

REVD ADAM SMALLBONE

Category: Good ☑ Bad ☐ Quirky ☐
Name: Revd Adam Smallbone
Actor: Tom Hollander

Character details

The Revd Adam Smallbone is the lead character in the BAFTA award winning BBC sitcom *Rev.* Somewhat hapless, the Revd Adam is the put-upon vicar of St Saviour in the Marshes – a fictional inner-city London parish. The sitcom *Rev.* sees Adam navigate the challenges of inner city life including dealing with middle class parents wanting to get their child into the good church school, a local crack addict, a crumbling church building and trying to avoid the wrath of Archdeacon Robert.

Score card:

Longevity	67%
Endearment	78%
Offence	56%
Vices	72%
Popularity	85%
Realism	98%

Revd Adam Smallbone – Rev.

Adam: 'Oh my God.'
Alex: 'Taking the Lord's name?'
Adam: 'It's a dialogue actually darling.'

Perhaps the greatest revolution in the depiction of on-screen Christians has been in the BAFTA award winning BBC sitcom *Rev*. The Revd Adam Smallbone is a kind of British anti-hero. He constantly fails to carry out his ideas, he smokes and hangs out regularly with local down-and-out Colin, he can't stop the unwanted advances of randy parishioner Adoha, fails to flirt successfully with the attractive head teacher at the local C of E school and he never satisfies the exacting requirements of the machiavellian Archdeacon Robert. A mass of contradictions, in some respects Revd Adam Smallbone is a walking disaster. And that's why we love him. He encapsulates everything we love in a character – not arrogant, well-meaning, tries hard and ultimately very flawed, Adam Smallbone is truly a vicar who is 'one of us'. Whenever he gets something right, it is despite himself. In this the writers have encapsulated very well what it is to be a Christian – despite not being Christians themselves.

Rev. updated the church-based sitcom from the now archaic seeming 1960s comedy *All Gas and Gaiters* in the same way Armando Iannucci updated political comedy *Yes Minister* with *The Thick of It*. Like *The Thick of It*, *Rev.* was created in consultation with real insiders – Revd Richard Coles among them. The result is a smoking, swearing vicar with a successful lawyer wife and an active sex life – exploding people's perceptions of what the clergy are like. People perceive the clergy a little like they do their school teachers. As a child it was always a shock to see one's teacher doing something ordinary like shopping – surely they lived in the school? In the same way people seem not to grow up about their view of the clergy – they assume that they don't have a life outside the wearing of funny frocks and intoning of boring prayers. This is what makes it so funny in the first episode of *Rev.* when Adam finally can't turn the other cheek any more with the rude builders who catcall him: he rips off his dog collar and shouts 'Fuck off!' – and we on our sofas cheer and breathe a sigh of relief: 'He is human after all.'

Rev. has achieved that rare accolade of public *and* church popularity – previously enjoyed by *All Gas and Gaiters* in the 1960s. *Rev.* watching parties sprang up in theological colleges up and down the country while the national press gave it rave reviews.

Revved up

One of the curious things about the times in which we are living is that where *The Vicar of Dibley* in its heyday attracted an audience of 15 million viewers, popular sitcom *Rev.* attracted an average audience of just 2 million in 2014. Although the audience figures for television are much smaller in this current age of multiple channels (as opposed to the 4 channels I grew up with) the commentariat is huge! In the 1990s one would look to a television critic in a broadsheet to get some opinion on a programme. Now, everyone is a critic. Thousands of tweets and many blog posts and articles in the mainstream media were written in

The 'good'

response to *Rev.* during the third series, which aired in 2014.

Television is a much more central part of our culture in our current times than it was in the past. It is watched perhaps by smaller audiences but in an interesting contrast it is commented upon much more as an art form – in a similar way in which critics have always written about films, theatre and music. Given the outburst of interest in, and comment on, *Rev.* I was intrigued to see what previous generations thought of such influential church-based comedies as 1960s classic *All Gas and Gaiters* and *The Vicar of Dibley* in the 1990s, so I did a search of the archive of the *Church Times*. In the entire archive (which goes back to 1863) I found only 14 articles referring to *The Vicar of Dibley* – most of which were small paragraphs in the television reviews – and 20 articles referring to *All Gas and Gaiters*, half of which were published since 2010.

MORE TV VICAR?

It seems that the previous generation deemed television programmes to be trivial and not worthy of column inches in a respectable newspaper such as the *Church Times*, whereas now, everyone has an opinion on it. In contrast, a search of the archive for articles on *Rev.* (which has only aired since 2010) threw up 15 articles – most of which were features. People today view television as a true art form. The birth of the DVD box set has invited more analysis of programmes and more niche fan clubs than ever – couple this with the ease of publishing your own views on social media and suddenly everyone and their dog is talking about it!

The vast majority of comments about *Rev.* during the third series came not from the general public – who simply enjoyed watching a well-made, well-acted comedy drama – but from Christians and clergy. Any programme which focuses on its own self-contained world (like the Church of England) is going to attract comment from people of that world – and now, with easy reach of twitter via our smartphones, the airwaves buzzed, particularly during the slightly edgier third series which dealt with such topics as gay marriage and paedophilia.

With so much comment flying around, the Christian Research Network surveyed 1,943 practising Christians about their views on *Rev.* – 65% of them had watched the programme (unsurprisingly, clergy were 30% more likely to have watched it[21]). Just as my friend Revd Alice watched *The Vicar of Dibley* while at theological college in the 1990s, I myself watched *Rev.* together with fellow ordinands (trainee priests) at my college. What I think is intriguing is that I first watched *Rev.* just as I was beginning to explore the possibility of ordination: so I was watching it as a lay person.

The 'good'

I loved it, I found it hilarious and moving and quite a helpful look into what the life of an ordained minister might be like (particularly in the inner city). Amazingly, it didn't put me off. Watching it now, knowing that I will be in the same role as Revd Adam Smallbone, does feel qualitatively different. It's not that I enjoy watching it any less, it's more that I laugh at different things. The excellent research and 'insider knowledge' is evident, but also I hide behind a cushion a bit more. It is a bit close to home. I think for some clergy, *Rev.* has operated as a bit of a therapy session – naming the challenges and difficulties of ministry: 'Lord, you didn't call me to be an accountant.' For others, it has been just too close to home – I know of some who simply can't bring themselves to watch it because it is 'too real'. Some have been angry with it, either irritated with Adam Smallbone's character or annoyed at the lack of reference to God in the programme:

> 'The BBC might like a pathetic, wimpy vicar who swears like a trooper and has the same values as the dominant elites and mobs of our culture. But I prefer a vicar of Christ.'[22]

As with any controversial programme, opinion is divided. Television does shape people's views – earlier I explored the impact of *The Vicar of Dibley* on views of women's ministry. Some see the programme *Rev.* as perpetuating the idea of the decline of the church in England. James Mumford wrote a comment piece in the *Guardian* declaring:

> 'You love *Rev.* I love *Rev.* Everyone loves *Rev.* That's why the hit BBC comedy is so pernicious.'[23]

Damning praise indeed! Mumford sees *Rev.* as insidiously perpetuating the idea of the church being in terminal decline. When asked to comment on the programme, the Archbishop of Canterbury, Justin Welby, felt he had to qualify what he said:

> 'The show amusingly depicts some of the challenges facing clergy up and down the country. But while it's great entertainment, it doesn't truly tell the whole story. I have a friend who runs a growing church in Reading city centre, filled with young people with no church background; I have another friend who has had to plan two new churches because his congregation is bursting at the seams. Other churches have few people but great impact, again with visionary and inspiring leadership. As with all of life, the picture is complex, but I see plenty of struggle and plenty of grounds for celebration. Therefore, while *Rev.* is great viewing, it doesn't depress me quite as much as you might think!'[24]

Most of the discomfort with *Rev.* comes from evangelicals in the Church of England. This is hardly surprising given that the Adam Smallbone character is depicted as a liberal catholic (i.e. more high church) and the consultants for the programme are from that part of the church spectrum. Indeed, in the first series, the 'trendy' evangelical HTB (Holy Trinity Brompton) style of church is mercilessly lampooned when a local vicar borrows Adam's church for a while and they install a smoothie bar and sound system.

Where some decry the lack of God's involvement in *Rev.*, Julia Raeside writing in the *Guardian* enjoyed its lack of cynicism about belief:

The 'good'

'Just when it seemed comedy went increasingly hand-in-hand with atheism, along came this contemporary sitcom which refuses to discount the possibility of god/God. Thank the Lord, because I can't think of a comedy since *The Vicar of Dibley* in which the protagonist has been allowed to believe in God without cynicism. Adam talks to "him" in a series of Peep Show-style voiceovers that don't strain to be ideological. And when he does seem to be losing his faith (at the end of last year's Christmas special), it only further highlights his humanity.'[25]

Rev. has gone a long way towards demonstrating that priests are ordinary, fallible human beings. This has been a source of some fascination to those outside the church – the programme provides a Wizard of Oz-like peep behind the curtain to a strange world.

Often, when a programme containing a focus on faith becomes popular, Christians place a huge burden on that programme which can be completely unreasonable. James Mumford writes:

'From the outset, *Rev.*'s operating assumption is that faith is individual. The Rev Smallbone's prayer monologues are purely personal. Faith is not something held in common. Nor is it transformative. Which is, rightly or wrongly, what people of faith think it is. Perhaps the show's most wonderful character, the drug addict Colin, is a parishioner Adam is genuinely friends with. But there's never a question of faith freeing him from addiction.'

What Mumford fails to understand is that *Rev.* is not a documentary about the church, it is a comedy set in a church. He's expecting the comedy to do something for which it was never written in the first place. For comedy to work there needs to be a series of characters who don't change very much and who respond in funny ways to different scenarios. It is odd that Mumford seems to think that the faith depicted in *Rev.* is individual, when the show revolves around a small group of parishioners who come together regularly to express their faith. As for the complaint that Colin is not freed from his addiction by his faith – first, his faith is clearly a huge part of his life, he continues to attend church, and, in the final episode of series 3 we hear his own heartfelt prayers to God. Second, if Colin were completely freed of his addiction, then his character would have to change – which the rules of sitcom simply wouldn't allow.

I asked my friend Revd Kate Bruce who her favourite Christian character on television was; she responded 'Colin'. I laughed, and then I thought about it and realised, yes, Colin is a great Christian character with a real faith – a rare thing to see on television. How many vicars do you know who have said, 'Yeah, we've got a Colin in our congregation'?

Mumford goes on to suggest that *Rev.* would be more interesting if it contained an actual miracle – such as someone being unexpectedly healed after Adam prays for her.[26] He seems to think this would be more of an 'insider view' of the church. I can't give a better response to this critique than Jem Bloomfield's friend: 'Dr Mumford's paradigmatic example of a Christian version of *Rev.* seems to involve parlour trick-style miracles. That's strange.'[27]

The 'good'

When the *Only Fools and Horses* writers wrote an episode with Del Boy and Rodney finally becoming millionaires it destroyed the whole premise of the show and it was not long before they had to make them penniless again to reinstate the beloved sitcom in the hearts of the nation. Something very similar would have happened to *Rev.* had the miracle of Colin being freed of addiction occurred or a healing taken place in the congregation. The beauty of the programme is in Adam's continued service to his community *despite* not ever really seeing any tangible results. *Rev.*, then, very much represents the 'insider view' that Mumford is calling for, just, unfortunately, not his type of insider!

Because the detail in *Rev.* is so accurate, because it is a 'squirmfest' as Revd Stephen Cherry put it,[28] people have thought it is genuinely portraying the state of the Church of England today. This is like expecting *Holby City* to be representative of life in the NHS or what happens to a single family on *EastEnders* to be the norm for everybody. Although it is a side-effect of a good programme that it feels accurate, it is not the point of *Rev.* The point of *Rev.* is to be a great comedy drama – something that was recognised when it was awarded a BAFTA in 2011. It remains to be seen what kind of impact the programme might have on views of the Church of England in the country at large. My suspicion is that most of the programme's Christian critics think that the general public care much more than they do in reality about the state of the Church of England today.

What's going on here?

'The church is still a place where people put the emotions that won't go anywhere else.'
— Rowan Williams quoting a former student[29]

There remains a fascination in public life with anyone who chooses to dedicate their lives to something that doesn't make money or win you fame. Christians, when portrayed well in the media, reflect part of this fascination. This quotation from Rowan Williams, I think, shows what was going on in *Broadchurch* – the 'emotions' that needed to be dealt with by a whole grieving community had to be dealt with by the church, there was nowhere else to go.

The character Bird in *Bluestone 42* is fascinated with Padre Mary – why would she choose to do this job? Underlying nearly every episode of *Rev.* is the question 'Why?' Why would someone choose to do a job like this with so little reward? This is the mystery of faith to people on the outside – it makes no sense. To quote scripture, 'God chose what is foolish in the world to shame the wise; God chose what is weak in the world to shame the strong.' (1 Cor. 1:27)

In the same speech I quoted from above, Rowan Williams says:

> 'I believe we are living in a society which is uncomfortably haunted by the memory of religion and doesn't quite know what to do with it, and I believe we are living in a society which is religiously plural and confused but not therefore necessarily hostile.'[30]

We can see this quite clearly in these few portrayals I have looked at here. The memory of religion lingers in British society. Occasionally the remembered faith re-enters the public sphere – notably on Remembrance Sunday but also events such as the Queen's Jubilee and the Royal Wedding or whenever a crisis hits a community. Slowly the church seems to be regaining its permission to be there, to have something legitimate to say.

This idea of religion (or, in this instance, the Church of England) 'haunting' society comes across in a curious comment in a recent report on the religious output of the BBC:

> 'Though both *Songs of Praise* on BBC One and *Sunday Worship* on Radio 4 have been a feature of the schedules for quite literally a lifetime, it always seems slightly surprising when the pattern of family viewing on TV, and news and magazine programmes on radio, are interrupted by a religious service. *It feels at the same time to be slightly anachronistic, and yet strangely reassuring.*' – Stuart Prebble (my emphasis)[31]

It is not altogether different from the way people feel about the Shipping Forecast on Radio 4. There is no real reason in the twenty-first century for the Shipping Forecast to be broadcast on the radio – sailors have very sophisticated equipment now for navigating the seas. Yet every time the broadcasting of this British institution is threatened there is total uproar – in 1995 there was a proposal to move the broadcast by just 12 minutes to a new slot that resulted in a debate in parliament! Hendy writes in a book on the history of Radio 4:

> 'The Shipping Forecast remained on air for no reason other than it is still wanted by many thousands of people who had no logical purpose in listening to it – other than the most basic purpose of all, of course, which was to make life a little bit richer in some intangible way.'[32]

The same could perhaps be said of the church – and especially the Church of England. People still want it, they still want to see it on their televisions, they just don't quite know why.

Our response

How do you feel about these realistic portrayals? Is it wrong to have a vicar character saying the 'F' word on television or is it refreshingly accurate?

If you are uncomfortable about these portrayals, ask yourself why. Is it because they are true? Is it because they present a version of a Christian that you don't recognise to be orthodox?

Perhaps what is more important is not your own personal response to this – whether positive or negative – but the effect these portrayals are having in the wider public consciousness. Slowly the church is shaking off its fusty image, slowly the public are accepting that Christians and in particular clergy are 'one of us' and know how to have fun. One has only to look at the response to the YouTube video of the Revd Kate Bottley's 'flash mob' dance at a wedding at which she was presiding[33] to see this shift of attitudes taking place. The video went viral and the response ranged from disgust in some quarters of the church to delight in the general public that a vicar would be willing to do something like that. I know which response is probably more helpful for the church's image.

The 'bad'

The Exorcist has a lot to answer for!

I was buying some groceries when I was at theological college and the man behind the counter asked me if I'd had a good day and I replied that I had, as I had finished an essay. He asked me what I was studying and I said, 'I'm training to be a priest' and his first response (and this is not the first time I have had this kind of comment) was, 'Do you get to go ghost catching then?' Movies like *The Exorcist* have left their mark on a whole generation with regard to their mental images of what a priest is. I said the word 'priest' and this man thought immediately of exorcism – not of anything else. The term 'priest' is nearly always associated with Catholicism. I've been asked a lot if I'm training to be a Roman Catholic priest – I have to say, 'No, they don't let women be priests yet'! The fire and brimstone priest character – whether Roman Catholic or a Protestant bible basher – is an enduring one in the popular imagination.

Comedy down the centuries has often been about

reversals and strange juxtaposition. Comedy writer Kevin Bleyer says: '.... much of comedy is contrasting two unlikely things and extending the metaphor beyond practicality.'[1] The humour is to be found in behaviour that is the opposite of that expected. Often our pagan festivals had elements of reversal – on May Day villages would crown someone 'Lord of Misrule' for the day and men would dress as women. Shakespeare knew all about this, filling his comedies with cross-dressing and people acting out of character for comic effect – like Malvolio in *Twelfth Night* strutting his stuff in his yellow garters. Comedians in our present age have exploited the trope of the fire and brimstone cleric by making that person from the Church of England – a hilarious reversal of expectation. The Church of England vicar of popular imagination is liberal, woolly, left-wing and nice – reverse these expectations and you end up with a great comic creation.

REVD BERNICE WOODALL

Category: Good ☐ **Bad** ☑ **Quirky** ☐
Name: Revd Bernice Woodall
Actor: Reece Shearsmith

Character details

Revd Bernice Woodall is the Church of England vicar of fictional creepy town Royston Vasey in the comedy series *The League of Gentlemen* written by Jeremy Dyson, Mark Gatiss, Steve Pemberton and Reece Shearsmith. Many of the female parts are played by male actors with Bernice the vicar played by Reece Shearsmith. Bernice doesn't believe in God or the Bible but enjoys berating people for their sins and frightening them about hell or humiliating them in the confessional booth. She has virtually no redeeming features, although, in the Christmas special we discover a childhood trauma which may have contributed to her twisted personality: this doesn't excuse her outrageous hatred for others, however!

Score card:

Longevity	15%
Endearment	0%
Offence	99%
Vices	98%
Popularity	50%
Realism	2%

The League of Gentlemen

'Some people call this "theatre in education", I call it "AIDS in a van".'
— Revd Bernice Woodall, *The League of Gentlemen*,
Series 1, Episode 4

Dark comedy *The League of Gentlemen* charts the events of a small town set in the brooding hills of Lancashire called Royston Vasey (incidentally, the real name of comedian Roy 'Chubby' Brown) and its collection of odd characters. What is so disturbing about the programme is the almost-believability of the place. The town is set in the present day with recognisable features such as a church, a job centre, a local taxi company and a school. Its characters are almost believable too, the woman who runs the Job Club, the ladies who volunteer at the charity shop, the butcher and so on. But five minutes into an episode, you realise that all is not quite right, although you can't quite put your finger on it. Royston Vasey does have one thing in common with Dibley: it has a woman priest:

> Revd Bernice Woodall [reading the bible]: 'And he will give strength to legs that are weak and arms that tremble. The crippled will throw down their crutches and leap up and down in praise of his grace.' Huh. Doesn't say they need five car parking spaces outside Safeway's now does it? They're always empty, I only nipped in for five minutes to get a bottle of Taboo! I come out and the bugger's clamped. I said to the man, would it have made

a difference if I had a stick and a limp? Ramps outside libraries, AND THEIR TOILETS ARE MASSIVE! Hymn number 513: 'Glad that I live am I!'

The Revd Bernice Woodall perhaps is the most evil Church of England character ever imagined. She is a character straight out of a horror film. Every bit of this 'sermon' is completely opposite to what she, as a priest, should be saying. It is vile, shocking and horrific, but curiously, therein lies the humour.

We are, perhaps, used to evil nun characters, but these are always Catholic and are born out of people's experiences of being shouted at by nuns in convent schools. *The League of Gentlemen* was first on television in 1999, not that long after the first women priests were ordained and certainly while the loveable Revd Geraldine Granger (of Dibley) was

still on air. Bernice is another woman vicar, from the good old woolly C of E – yet she is absolutely full of bile and fire and brimstone. It is so jarring as to be funny. If Geraldine Granger is 'too blooming nice' then Bernice Woodall is her exact opposite, 'too bastardy evil'! It seems as if the writers of The League of Gentlemen took the opposite approach from Richard Curtis (The Vicar of Dibley) imagining a woman priest character and rather than make her loveable, dreamt up the most hateful character they could. She has so few redeeming features as a character that in the Christmas special, where you discover that she had a childhood trauma (her mother was kidnapped by the terrifying Papa Lazarous) you still have no sympathy for her (although it might provide some clue as to why she is such a twisted individual).

The Church of England stereotype is the limp handshake, liberal, friendly, likeable sort. Bernice Woodall is the kind of person who has a crushing handshake, is fiercely right wing and simply downright mean:

> 'I welcome this new road and every blast of carbon monoxide it brings. If God meant us to walk everywhere, he wouldn't have given us Little Chefs.' – Revd Bernice Woodall, The League of Gentlemen

And that's why it's funny. There is something curiously hilarious about an evil, fire and brimstone vicar character precisely because one can't imagine anyone is really like that in the Church of England. I guess those of us who are Anglican should take it as some kind of compliment!

DAVID MITCHELL'S 'EVIL' VICAR

Category: Good ☐ **Bad** ☑ **Quirky** ☐
Name: Unnamed 'evil' vicar
Actor: David Mitchell

Character details

The evil man, 'still unaccountably a vicar' is one of three characters (the other two are a waiter and a menswear salesman) who behave in the opposite way to that expected. In this sketch from *That Mitchell and Webb Look*, David Mitchell plays a Church of England vicar 'gone bad' who is visited by a fresh faced 'seeker' couple who are wondering where that 'nice lady vicar in the colourful jumper' that they met last week has gone. He forces them out of his church in a mock exorcism before complaining that they didn't leave any money in the collection plate.

Score card:

Longevity	10%
Endearment	0%
Offence	85%
Vices	95%
Popularity	85%
Realism	15%

That Mitchell and Webb Look

'Who the hell did you think you were going to say "Hi" to? The Lord your God? Because I'm not sure you've lived lives worthy of His attention.'
— Evil Vicar character, *That Mitchell and Webb Look*, Series 3, Episode 4, BBC 2009

This evil vicar trope can be found in other places too. Mitchell and Webb in their sketch show have a series of characters who are 'still unaccountably x' – in the show variously a waiter, a menswear assistant and, of course, a vicar. A young middle class couple wander into a church hoping to meet the 'friendly lady vicar in the colourful jumper' they saw the other week. When they share that they are a 'bit spiritual' they are confronted by this tirade from a terrifying cassocked cleric:

'Not particularly religious. Interested. Spiritual. Are you testing me Satan? ... aren't you all entitled to your half-arsed musings on the divine? You've thought about eternity for 25 minutes and think you've come to some interesting conclusions? Well let me tell you, I stand with 2000 years of darkness and bafflement and hunger behind me. My kind have harvested the souls of a million peasants and I couldn't give a ha'penny jizz for your internet-assembled philosophy.'

As the sketch goes on the couple are hounded out of the building by said cleric brandishing a crucifix. This sketch unashamedly borrows from the idea of a hysterical priest

The 'bad'

conducting an exorcism in a horror film. Again, it is the juxtaposition of the friendliness of the couple and the complete lack of friendliness on the part of the vicar that is so funny. His response to them is out of all proportion to their request (as Kevin Bleyer says 'extending the metaphor beyond all practicality'). What is interesting about this particular sketch is the glee with which we watch it.

This relates to the constant Christian need to be 'nice' which is played upon so well in *The Vicar of Dibley* but also to a degree with Padre Mary Greenstock in *Bluestone 42*. James Cary, the comedy writer, sees the constant need to be nice to idiots as the engine of the comedy in *The Vicar of*

Dibley and also uses it to comic effect in his own sitcom as Mary squirms to avoid swearing.

This sketch is unsurprisingly, and slightly disturbingly, popular with clergy, although, in some respects this is not altogether different from the secret wish of people who work in customer service to say horrible things to their customers, or for teachers to be vile to the pupils who drive them mad. There is an added frisson, however, because of the Christian label and the expectations of behaviour on Christians to love one another (John 13:34).

I suspect that David Mitchell and Robert Webb had no idea what they created when they wrote this sketch: great therapy for fed-up clergy!

THE BABY-EATING BISHOP OF BATH & WELLS

Category: Good ☐   Bad ☑   Quirky ☐
Name: The Baby-Eating Bishop of Bath & Wells
Actor: Ronald Lacey

Character details

The Baby-Eating Bishop of Bath and Wells is a satirical character in the historical sitcom *Blackadder* (whose writers included Ben Elton and Richard Curtis). Although he only appears in one episode ('Money', from 1986) his character has been seared on the popular imagination – most probably because of his outrageously inappropriate epithet. He admits that he is a 'colossal pervert', and enjoys the company of prostitutes. He is angry when customers are unable to pay up, and also drowns babies in the christening font and then eats them later in the vestry – hence the delightful moniker.

Score card:

Longevity	80%
Endearment	0%
Offence	87%
Vices	99%
Popularity	95%
Realism	5%

Blackadder

'Never have I encountered such foul, mindless perversity. Have you considered a career in the church?'
— The Baby-Eating Bishop of Bath and Wells,
Blackadder episode 'Money', BBC 1986

The king of the character reversals is the Baby-Eating Bishop of Bath and Wells from *Blackadder*. His character only appears in one episode but has influenced a generation to snigger whenever they hear the real Bishop of Bath and Wells mentioned. This character is different from the two

we have just looked at in that he is not really proper C of E. The programme is set during the reign of Elizabeth I when the fluffy, friendly C of E was but a twinkle in Good Queen Bess's eye, and he is more of a satirical character than a straight reversal.

One of the wonderful things about *Blackadder* is the historical focus – many of the jokes are based on what we know about the past.[2] There is some confusion, as some characters really did exist, such as Queen Elizabeth, but many others are made up for the purposes of comedy. I hate to break it to you, but there was historically no 'Baby-Eating Bishop of Bath and Wells' – it was just a clever use of an already slightly funny Bishop's title to create a funny joke. For some reason, the Bishop of Bath and Wells has become a go-to comedy bishop character having been used elsewhere, such as in *Monty Python* and radio comedy *Absolute Power*. In *Blackadder* the character plays on what we know of the corruption that was evident in parts of the church at the time of the Reformation. He represents the extreme of this abuse of power in the church to great comic effect, saying to Blackadder at the end of the episode entitled 'Money':

> 'Never have I encountered such foul, mindless perversity. Have you considered a career in the church?'

The humour in his character is in his evident lack of regard for how people expect him to behave; he relishes his bad reputation and flaunts his principal vice (one of many) of being partial to eating babies. There are a number of comedic effects going on: the name is just funny, always stated in full, 'The Baby-Eating Bishop of Bath and Wells'. Second, we can delight in the lampooning of a historical period (much as in the same way we might laugh at Monty Python's *Life of Brian*), we can say 'Oh, yes, wasn't it terrible in those days. Wasn't the church corrupt!' Thirdly, there is an element of what we saw in the character of Bernice Woodall and in David Mitchell's evil vicar – the idea of an utterly corrupt evil priest is funny because it is so unlikely.

It's difficult to be offended by such characters as they are so extreme as to be unbelievable – their unbelievability is essential to the humour.

Mockery versus satire

So far, these 'bad' characters we have looked at have been largely a bit of fun – and also a slightly backhanded compliment to Christians. An area of great influence in popular culture is stand-up comedy. Back in the 1990s comedy was declared the 'new rock and roll' and many stand-up comedians today regularly fill stadiums and make millions (such as Michael McIntyre and Peter Kay). In recent years, many of the most prominent stand-up comics have had something in common – they are nearly all atheists and are not afraid to talk about it or to poke fun at belief and believers. What is going on with this? Should Christians be offended? Does Christianity have 'broader shoulders' than other religions?

Atheist stand-up comedy

Three of the most influential stand-up comedians whose shows contain a lot of anti-religion material are Ricky Gervais, Tim Minchin and Jimmy Carr. Their targets are the Roman Catholic church, other 'organised' religion, right-wing and unthinking believers and biblical literalism. To many devout Christians, these are perfectly legitimate targets. Abuse of power must be challenged: it's even a Christian imperative, so to target abuses of power with comedy should be acceptable to all Christians. But do these particular comedians go too far?

Here's Ricky Gervais on the Bible:

> 'The thing about rumour is, if someone's written it down everyone will believe it. You can have the most far-fetched, made-up, impossible, illogical bollocks, and if it's in print, someone will believe it. Just look at the Bible.'
>
> — Ricky Gervais, *Fame*, 2007

The problem with Gervais' attitude to the bible is that he thinks all Christians have the same take on it – he effectively assumes all Christian believers are biblical literalists. He said, tellingly, in an interview with Piers Morgan on CNN:

> 'I just believe that the earth was created over 4 and a half billion years and not by design over 6 days.'[3]

A lot of Christians, myself included, could respond, 'Me too' to that statement. The 'believers' that he is having a go at are very thin on the ground in the UK. Steve Punt pointed this out in the documentary *Are you having a laugh?*

> 'The comedy is an aggressive reply to the aggressive nature of American creationism...it is a bit of a

cheat because there aren't many creationists or fundamentalists in Britain.'[4]

It is a cheat. It is also incredibly arrogant. Gervais' comedy assumes that everyone in the audience agrees with him: 'We are the clever ones and isn't everyone else stupid?' Tim Minchin feels a similar sense of superiority:

> 'I think the trouble with being a critical thinker or an atheist, or a humanist is that you're right. And it's quite hard being right in the face of people who are wrong without sounding like a fuckwit. People go, "Do you think the vast majority of the world is wrong", well, yes. I don't know how to say that nicely, but yes.'

Who is the fundamentalist now? I think, for me, it's the sense of superiority that offends me more than what they say about religion. Many of their claims against 'religion' are actually against the abuses of religion, which is fair game for a challenge, but assuming that you're right and everyone else is wrong and that your entire audience agrees with you – that's pure arrogance and precisely one of the complaints they level at fundamentalist believers.

Things usually get more uncomfortable for Christians when the person of Jesus is the focus of the humour. Jimmy Carr has some select one-liners:

'If we are all God's children, what's so special about Jesus?'

'When I was a kid, I used to have an imaginary friend. I thought he went everywhere with me.

I could talk to him and he could hear me, and he could grant me wishes and stuff too. But then I grew up, and stopped going to church.'

'Jesus loves you... He's not "in love" with you.'

These are quite witty but they're also very smug – although smugness is a definite part of Carr's comedy persona. I asked Christian comedian Paul Kerensa how far was too far, he said, 'For me it gets trickier the closer to the cross you get. I've heard comedians doing gags about Jesus, and I'm a bit on edge then, but if it's about the cross or jokes about the crucifixion, which I've heard very rarely, then generally you're going out to shock more than anything. So I think, for me, that's where I'd draw the line.'

Jimmy Carr was raised a Catholic and believed until he was 26. He said in an interview with *Digital Spy*:[5]

'Actually my show has no message. That's one of the key things with my stand-up. There's no message in it.'

'You wouldn't believe how little I care about what you believe. Good luck, if it makes you happy – great. But I'm not trying to change your opinion on anything.'

This is another assumption many atheist comedians make – that their position is 'neutral', that they're not 'forcing their beliefs on you' like Christians do. I do wonder, though, how much the sheer arrogance of some of these sets has made some people think, 'Oh yeah, people who are religious are all stupid'. I was in a taxi when at college and I got chatting with the driver and told him I was training to be a vicar. His response was, 'Hasn't all that stuff been disproved now, what with evolution and everything?' I had to then go through the laborious disentangling process that most thinking Christians have to do when faced with a comment like that. I told him that I believed that evolution was likely to be the way the earth was created but that I also believed in God. The problem is that nuanced thinking isn't funny: people who think in black and white terms are funny. So, on the whole, I choose not to be offended by this type of comedy as it describes a belief system that I don't subscribe to either.

There is a strong element of laziness in this kind of comedy. Speaking to both comedy writer James Cary and comedian Paul Kerensa, we discussed how the issue is not always so much that the comedians are being offensive but more that they are offensively lazy in their comedy, as Paul told me:

'For a while, you couldn't go and see an Edinburgh festival show without a comedian saying, "I'm an atheist by the way" just to try and sound a bit more cool – almost like a calling card, like "if I don't say this I can't be a proper comedian". It's a fashion thing, it was a couple of years ago now, if someone said it now a critic would say "it's very 2008", it's no longer got an edginess to it. It'll probably come back but once one or two big name comedians have done it, then other people join in and people think, "Oh, this is what comedy is, this is how to be a bit edgy". The truth of it is that it is not that edgy because a lot of the people in the audience are thinking, "Fine, OK, if you think that" – I don't think they're really "sticking it to the man" as they think they are.'

Even some comedians have spotted this trend with Bridget Christie saying in one of her sets:

'I pretend to be a Catholic because there are not many Catholics on the circuit, there's lots of atheist comics on the circuit and I thought that I would pretend to be a Catholic and maybe that would boost my profile and maybe I'd get some publicity for it. But no one gave a shit really.'[6]

Paul shared this insight about stand-up comedy:

'Comedians are always trying to find the new "edge". When I started out in 2002, on the open mic scene every comedian was talking about sex in some way and then a year later it suddenly seemed that was not enough so it used to be paedophilia. Then about 4 years ago there was loads of misogyny, rape, horrible stuff but comedians trying to make jokes about the new taboo, which I think is a massive mistake. The audiences just want to laugh. In my job I'm hoping that most people in the audience have had as good a time as possible, whereas some comedians go in there thinking "I'm happy to alienate half the audience to try and get the people I want to to laugh". I think that doesn't really respect the audience in the same way as if you say "look, let's all have a good time, as much as possible". You can't please all the people all the time, but trying to be edgy all the time and trying to find this "new edge" is problematic for comedy generally. Also, where do you end up going? I'm now a rarity in that I'm on a comedy show and I'm clean: are clean comics the new edgy comics?'

So it seems the atheist onslaught on the comedy circuit is on the wane – which in turn will hopefully stop a certain sort of Christian bemoaning how we are 'persecuted' in the West.

Do your research!

Comedy works when people can recognise truth being revealed – it's why in recent years observational comedy has become so popular: there is real pleasure in realising 'that's so true!' Two other comedians who are known to be atheist but who have a slightly different approach to laughing about religion are Dara O'Briain and Eddie Izzard. They speak about what they know. Only someone who had been raised in the Church of England could have so accurately spoofed Anglican congregational singing like Eddie Izzard:

> 'There's something weird, something phenomenally dreary about Christian singing. The Gospel singers are the only singers that just go crazy, joyous and it's fucking amazing! And it's born out of kidnapping, imprisonment, slavery, murder, all of that – and this joyous singing! And the Church of England, well, all those sort of Christian religions, which is mainly Caucasian white people, with all the power and money – enough power and money to make Solomon

blush, and they're all singing, [dirge-like] "Oh, God, our hope in ages past, our hope for years..." They're the only groups of people that could sing, "Alleluia" without feeling like it's an "Alleluia!" thing, [drearily] "Alleluia, Alleluia, joyfully we lark about." '

— Eddie Izzard, *Dress to Kill*, 1998

This humour works in a different manner from the attack-dog comedians – this is in the 'it's funny because it's true' category. Dara O'Briain is another atheist comedian but again, he speaks of what he knows about, he doesn't try to convince people that believers are stupid, but rather shares some of his own experiences, such as being at a wedding between a Protestant and a Catholic and the resulting competition over who will say the Lord's Prayer 'correctly'. When challenged by some Christians about why he doesn't joke about Muslims he retorted 'my job is not to write you jokes about Muslims, I write about stuff I know, and I know about growing up Catholic'.[7]

This kind of humour is not going for the cheap shot but rather is born of experience or at least the comedian has some genuine engagement with the topic at hand. Eddie Izzard's comedy often uses biblical themes, in his recent show *Force Majeure*, for example, he gives a laugh-out-loud account of an exchange between Pontius Pilate and Jesus in the run-up to his crucifixion. 'Are you the King of the Jews?', asks a frustrated Pilate. 'Well, that's what *you've* said', comes the annoyingly evasive reply from Jesus. 'Grr!', says Eddie. Cue big laugh from the audience. Izzard is simply paraphrasing scripture and finding the humour therein. Writing for the Bible Society's blog, Ben Whitnall says that he'd love to go to a bible study with Eddie Izzard:

'If nothing else, Eddie Izzard actually *engages with Scripture.* That's got to be an improvement on leaving it shut away in splendid isolation. He gets that there's plenty of interesting stuff in the Bible, whether or not you're a Christian. And his playful approach means that he's often exploring more dimensions of Scripture than you'd get in a rushed "I know the right answer before I even start" reading.'[8]

For so long we have not felt it appropriate to laugh in our churches or to laugh at the bible and yet there is much humour in the bible. Jesuit priest James Martin has written a whole book on spirituality and humour. In it he speaks to biblical scholar Professor Amy-Jill Levine who points out that the great hyperbole in many of Jesus' parables was not only clever but intentionally funny: 'I suspect that the early readers found these stories hilarious, whereas we in a very different social setting miss the point entirely'.[9] In the same book Margaret Silf exclaims:

'Why do we sit so solemnly through all the stories about trying to take the splinter out of someone's eye when you have a plank in your own or about camels going through the eye of needles? So many ridiculously exaggerated characters and situations that no one could forget! Can't you see the tongue in Jesus's cheek? Or even the cheek in Jesus's tongue?'[10]

So Eddie Izzard is in a grand tradition of those early Christians who shared the hilarious stories of Jesus!

The 'bad'

Offence is good?

Politician and Roman Catholic Anne Widdecombe created a documentary[11] with atheist comedian Marcus Brigstocke asking the question of whether comedians are now going too far with their jokes about religion. This programme was triggered by the rise in comedians becoming more strident in their atheist views. Marcus Brigstocke says: 'I particularly like going after the aspect of religion I object to with comedy...there is a great amount about the Christian faith that I find horrible.' Anne Widdecombe retorts: 'I think comedy should keep its hands off things that are sacred'.

Anne's position is not too far from Paul Kerensa's view that things get difficult for Christians the closer you get to the cross. Mocking the evil things done in the name of religion or mocking comical clergy characters is fair game but once you get to the question of the actual beliefs held by Christians, there is potential for offence.

One of the problems with some of the comedy that focuses on the central tenets of the Christian faith is the lack of religious literacy in the general population. This can be demonstrated by the fact that many of the jokes in the originally scandalous Monty Python film *Life of Brian* rely on a good knowledge of the bible. Take, for instance, the joke with the misheard Sermon on the Mount:

Spectator 1:   I think it was 'Blessed are the cheesemakers'.

Mrs. Gregory: Aha, what's so special about the cheesemakers?

Gregory: Well, obviously it's not meant to be taken literally; it refers to any manufacturers of dairy products.[12]

For the joke to work, one has to know that Jesus said 'Blessed are the peacemakers' – but very few cinema-goers now would recognise that. Steve Punt points out the irony of this:

> 'I wonder whether some of the people who complained about it will actually now find themselves thinking "Do you know what, I rather long for the days when people knew enough about the bible to complain about the *Life of Brian*." '[13]

In the same documentary, this becomes clear as a particular sketch from comedy show *Goodness Gracious Me* is highlighted as the most offensive sketch to Christians. In the sketch a South Asian family who are doing their best to demonstrate their good 'English' credentials decide to go to church, when they go to receive communion, one of them brings out some mango chutney to put on the communion wafer. Anne Widdecombe says of this, in disgust: 'It wasn't one step too far: it was a mile too far.' The programme at the time received 62 formal complaints, including from representatives of the Church of England Archbishops' Council, which were upheld by the BBC, but it appears that the sketch writers were not aware of the high level of offence that they caused. Producer Anil Gupta says of the sketch, 'The intention was not to mock the tenets of Christianity.' The joke is actually about the family totally misunderstanding the strange religious ceremony of Holy Communion (and it *is* rather strange to the uninitiated) rather than actually mocking Holy Communion itself. I can see why some Christians would find this incredibly offensive, but for myself, I can see the ignorance behind the writing of the sketch. One could make an equally bad faux pas choosing a ritual from another religion to try and make a joke. As Steve Punt says in the same documentary: 'Unfortunately for the devout, religion is funny.'

That sketch went out on air in 2000 and the religious literacy and awareness of the general population has only declined further since then. No longer can we assume that there is a default level of background knowledge of Christianity as there was in the 1970s when *Life of Brian* caused such a scandal.

Those of us who are practising Christians, then, may still find ourselves from time to time offended by certain religious jokes – whether those that are deliberately offensive or those that are unintentionally offensive. Christian and comedy writer James Cary thinks this isn't a bad thing:

> 'It's good to be offended. When Christians are surprised by the bad language in the show [*Bluestone 42*] and I say "Are you offended by it?" and they say "Yes", I say "Good, it's good to be offended, I wouldn't talk like that!" I think people think erroneously they have a right not to be offended. Actually, offence is a good thing, as it shows you have a moral compass, it's prompting you that there might be something wrong here. Jesus tells stories, like the parable of the Good Samaritan – it's incredibly offensive if you're a Levite or a Priest and Jesus intentionally told that intending to offend them.'

Stand-up comedian Paul Kerensa agrees: 'a little bit of offence can go a long way to actually provoking us to certain ways of engaging with subject matter.' There is a very interesting discussion between Anne Widdecombe and Marcus Brigstocke about this issue of offence. In the end, Marcus states: 'If my comedy succeeds in preventing you from being a Christian, then we have a problem. And we don't have that problem in this country.'

This gets to the nub of the matter, a little bit of offence can be a good thing. It confirms that we have a conviction about something. This is most definitely not 'persecution', it is more simply a symptom of the religiously plural society in which we now live. Christianity's, or more accurately, Christendom's, loss of its monopoly on belief in Great Britain is perhaps no bad thing – it leads Christians to consider what it means (to use a phrase of Pope Benedict) to be a 'creative minority.'[14] We have a choice, we can get huffy about it or we can engage with the culture around us.

What's going on here?

We've seen television delighting in the religious stereotypes of the past: the fire and brimstone bible bashing preachers and corrupt leaders of the church. We've looked at stand-up comedy delighting in ridiculing unthinking Christian fundamentalists – tarring all believers with the same brush. What this demonstrates very clearly is the end of Christianity's hegemony in the UK. On the one hand, Christians can be flattered that the over-the-top role reversal characters like the Revd Bernice Woodall from *The League of Gentlemen* work precisely because they are so unlikely to exist in real life. On the other hand, people's general knowledge of the Christian faith and the bible is at such a low that offence is often caused unintentionally – such as through the Holy Communion sketch in *Goodness Gracious Me*, and jokes such as those made in *Life of Brian* produce a tumbleweed effect rather than gales of laughter. Consistent attacks on belief from atheist comedians have created a sense of pride in those who are atheist and an unhelpful arrogance that prevents dialogue. In comedy, black and white works where grey areas do not – comedians will always tackle the extremes of any position as that is where the humour is to be found. Hence many comedians go for the stereotype fundamentalist evangelical (who is usually American) for a cheap laugh.

It seems, from my conversation with comedian Paul Kerensa that the rampant atheism on the stand-up stage at least is on the wane – it's a tired joke now. Having said that, in some respects I think many of the comedians such as Ricky Gervais have done some damage in influencing a whole generation to think that anyone who is religious, and particularly anyone who identifies as Christian, is basically an idiot:

> 'Religion is what we had until we discovered what mental illness is.'
>
> — Frankie Boyle

This makes it a little more challenging to be a Christian and be open about it but the lack of knowledge of what Christians *actually* believe is an opportunity to put people right.

Our response

One of the greatest ironies of the mocking of Christian belief and of Christianity in the UK is that without

Christianity we probably wouldn't have such a healthy comedy scene and use of satire. Much of Jesus' teaching used the techniques of comedians such as hyperbole and juxtaposition to expose the misuse of power in his own society. Christianity is an inherently radical religion – its earliest creed 'Jesus is Lord' was a subversive reversal of the Roman declaration 'Caesar is Lord'. Stephen Fry in an interview when asked about the difference between British and American comedy also draws on our Catholic Christian roots:

> 'There is a sense of original sin in Europe (and this is a bizarre theory that I won't push to its limit) but when it comes to comedy it is satisfactorily, I think, obvious that the American comic hero is a wise-cracker, who is above his material and who is above the idiots around him ... whereas the British comedian wants to play the failure. All the great British comic heroes are people who want life to be better and on whom life craps from a terrible height and whose sense of dignity is constantly compromised by the world letting them down. They are a failure, they are brought up to expect empire and decency and being able to wear a blazer in public and everyone around them just laughs.'[15]

Built in to the British psyche is this sense of self-deprecation – which one doesn't find so much in other countries. The self-deprecation is fundamentally linked to our sense of humour. This played out marvellously in the opening ceremony of the London 2012 Olympic Games with the Queen quite happily performing as herself with James Bond, with the big joke at the end of the short film being that she parachuted into the Olympic Stadium. Chinese commentators were reportedly stunned into silence in incomprehension[16] while the rest of the UK cheered and laughed. That our head of state was willing to take part in such a gag says a lot about our culture.

So our response to these 'bad' portrayals? Let's be British about it. If something offends you, good! It shows that you do care about what you believe. Be grateful that we live in a culture which encourages satire, encourages the challenge of misuse of power – it's following in the tradition of Jesus Christ.

The 'quirky'

Father Dougal: God, Ted, I heard about those cults.
Everyone dressing in black and saying Our Lord's going to
come back and judge us all.
Father Ted: No ... Dougal, that would be us now.
You're talking about Catholicism, there.[1]

There are some portrayals of Christians on television
that almost defy categorisation. These are recognisable
stereotypes or caricatures but are neither wholly 'good'
(accurate or wholesome) nor wholly 'bad'. These I have put
into the category of 'quirky' since they do not fit anywhere
else. They are the mis-shapes – the entertaining, odd
boundaries of religion on television. Some are stereotypes
taken to something of an extreme, some are purely surreal
but they still say something about the enduring interest in
the strange world of faith and particularly Christian faith in
popular culture.

Father Ted

A remote island off the coast of Ireland, a sprawling
parochial house, an eccentric tea-obsessed housekeeper,
one elderly alcoholic priest, one hard-pressed well-meaning
priest, one bemused assistant priest – not necessarily the
basis for one of the best sitcoms of the last thirty years.

The 'quirky'

Graham Linehan and Arthur Mathews' 1990s comedy about the life of three priests living in the same house on a small island is perhaps, even more than *The Vicar of Dibley*, the most beloved programme ever to have starred characters who are priests, There has been a contestant on *Mastermind* who had *Father Ted* as his specialist subject, there is an annual Father Ted festival in Kilfenora (the location of Craggy Island Parochial House) attended by hundreds of fans in costume, re-enacting scenes from the show, and there are regular repeats of the programme on television, twenty years since it was first broadcast. Why is there such affection for this comedy about priests? What kind of impact has it had culturally?

Father Ted is almost uncategorisable. There are elements of the traditional sitcom (it was filmed, when not on location, in front of a live studio audience) but the world it depicts is both familiar and surreal. The characters are not even necessarily stereotypes, they are like characters from a parallel universe; they have a cartoon-like quality which I think is possibly the reason for the affection people have for them. 'We wanted to create this odd world that was outside of everything'[2] says Graham Linehan, co-creator of *Father Ted*. The programme is set on a remote island and is about the life of three priests living in a parochial house together – a world about which no one actually knows anything so the writers had free rein to create ridiculous storylines and surreal scenes. The writers draw on some common experiences of certain priest characters, our basic (but limited) knowledge of what priests do (e.g. drinking tea with parishioners) and then fill in the gaps with all sorts of hilarious capers.

I remember watching the first series with glee while

I was still in my Roman Catholic girls' school in the sixth form. It struck a chord with us as so many of the priests we encountered at school were like versions of those depicted in *Father Ted*. I distinctly remember one priest being presented with a bottle of whisky at an end of term mass. He put it on the altar at the end of the service and there was a procession out of the school hall in the final hymn. Half way down the aisle, he stopped the procession and rushed back to retrieve his precious whisky before leaving the hall. I'm not saying he was exactly like Father Jack, but...

Linehan and Mathews struck comedy gold by making a sitcom about a world none of us know anything about apart from the surface details. This gave them scope to have a bit of fun with stereotypes at the same time as creating a self-contained world that they could play with, rather like a cartoon, where people could get bashed over the head with a frying pan and come up smiling – or in Mrs Doyle's case, regularly fall out of the window!

FATHER TED CRILLY, FATHER DOUGAL McGUIRE & FATHER JACK HACKETT

Category: Good ☐ Bad ☐ Quirky ☑

Names: Father Ted Crilly, Father Dougal McGuire & Father Jack Hackett

Actors: Dermot Morgan, Ardal O'Hanlon & Frank Kelly

Character details

Father Ted is the sitcom's beleaguered everyman character; he's a man who seems to have found himself in the priesthood by accident. So is Father Dougal who is dim-witted, childlike and has no idea what he is doing. Father Jack is an old-school fire and brimstone priest with a penchant for women and alcohol who drinks to numb the pain of being trapped with two idiots on a remote Irish island.

Score card:

Longevity	98%
Endearment	99%
Offence	61%
Vices	95%
Popularity	97%
Realism	32%

Father Ted, Channel 4, 1995–98

> **Father Ted:** Okay, one last time, Dougal. These [he points to some plastic cows on the table] are small; but the ones out there [pointing at some cows out of the window] are far away...

> **Father Jack Hackett:** Drink! Feck! Arse! Girls!

Just as I suggested that *The Vicar of Dibley* acted as a Trojan horse in Middle England to change perceptions of women in ministry, something similar took place with *Father Ted*, particularly in Ireland. Precisely because *Father Ted* is set in this strange cartoony parallel universe it had the effect of presenting the church as being exactly that – completely unrelated to the real world and, therefore, irrelevant. This was actually very radical in a country in which the church had held sway for far longer and in a different manner from England. Writer Graham Linehan in a recent interview describes an article that stated: 'Ted basically lanced a boil for Irish people. Also, another guy told me that hardliners on both sides of the Northern Ireland problem loved it ... it brought a lot of people together, and I think that was only possible because we didn't take the hard-edged satirical approach. We were just silly.'[3] There's nothing like a bit of ridiculous humour to burst the bubble of fragile authority – propaganda in the British Isles has always worked along those lines.

What is fascinating is that those who are in the church or sympathetic to the church absolutely loved and still love

this way to
the Stump of
St. Kevin

or this
way

But this way
to be sure

CB

Father Ted (I still use the line 'that would be an ecumenical matter'[4] to get out of awkward situations) and those that are hostile to the church absolutely love *Father Ted*. Declan Downey, the director, says in a documentary about the show: 'The anti-church thing that people say it has, that was never there for me and I don't think it was there for the guys … but it struck a chord. I remember priests coming and sitting in our parlour for four or five hours drinking cups of tea … it was in our psyche, we knew about that stuff.' Like Dara O'Briain, these comedians were writing about what they knew and in the process became accidental satirists.

If it *is* satire (or at least a form of satire) it is extremely affectionate. The characters are almost all endearing, even the horrendous Father Jack, with whom we end up sympathising because he is stuck living with such idiots: 'How did that gobshite get on the television?'[5]

Each of the main characters, writer Graham Linehan points out, is something of a caricature of people's perceptions of the Irish:

> 'We were certainly sick of the clichés about Ireland – even the nice ones – so it felt good to bend and stretch and exaggerate those stereotypes until they became caricatures. Mrs Doyle is a caricature of our alleged friendliness, Jack is a caricature of our supposed capacity for drink and Dougal is a caricature of our perceived hilarious and delightful light-headedness, God bless us.'[6]

The characters are also, perhaps, caricatures of types of religious belief. Dougal represents pure ignorance, a blissful lack of awareness about anything to do with the soul:

Dougal: Do you believe in an afterlife?
Ted: Well, Dougal, what would you say? Considering that for the last twenty years I've been walking round administering the sacraments and being a general type of spiritual light in people's lives …
Dougal: You're sort of uncertain?
Ted: No, in fact, I'm actually the opposite of uncertain. Generally speaking, priests tend to have a fairly strong belief in the afterlife.

The 'quirky'

Dougal: I wish I had your faith, Ted.
Ted: Dougal, how did you get into the Church? Was it, like, collect twelve crisp packets and become a priest?[7]

I think one of the reasons that Dougal is so loveable (apart from his childlike qualities) is that he is an example of someone who is supposed to be professional who genuinely has no clue what he is doing. Oliver Burkeman writes this of people in authority and of institutions:

> 'One of the most fundamental yet still under-appreciated truths of human existence ... is this: everyone is totally just winging it, all the time.
>
> Institutions – from national newspapers to governments and political parties – invest an enormous amount of money and effort in denying this truth. The facades they maintain are crucial to their authority, and thus to their legitimacy and continued survival. We need them to appear ultra-competent, too, because we derive much psychological security from the belief that somewhere, in the highest echelons of society, there are some near-infallible adults in charge.
>
> In fact, though, everyone is totally just winging it.'[8]

Dougal absolutely represents this truth. It is strangely reassuring, the silly idea that someone would allow Dougal to be a priest. It acts as a kind of catharsis for those of us who suffer from impostor syndrome (the panic that one day you'll be found out as a fraud):

Dougal: God, Ted, I heard about those cults. Everyone dressing in black and saying Our Lord's going to come back and judge us all.

Ted: No ... Dougal, that would be us now. You're talking about Catholicism, there.[9]

The character of Father Ted is in the tradition of many comedy greats, always having a hair-brained scheme that never quite comes to fruition – we spend the whole time feeling sorry for him, and although he's an idiot, he's the most normal of the idiots and the one with whom we most readily identify. Ted, like Dougal, manages to get the religion part of his job completely wrong. Writer Arthur Mathews says of him:

> 'The only time we ever see Ted pray is when he's in terrible trouble and he calls on God in the last resort. But he always gets it wrong, he even offers God money to help them get rid of Father Stone.'[10]

Ted has a naïve, Homer Simpson-like attitude to faith and the humour is in the fact that a priest really should know better. We take some delight in this: that even a priest tries to bargain with God. Ted is a materialist and can never quite sit comfortably with the ascetic demands of being a priest: his fantasy is to be living a life of luxury, with women and fast cars. He even tries to fix a raffle to win a car. I suspect there is a little bit of Ted in all of us.

Father Jack represents the fire and brimstone approach to religion. Jack gets sadistic pleasure from the suffering of others and in some respects is the most satirical of all the characters. His character is extreme but imagined from real experiences of nasty priests. He represents the worst of the abuses of religion. Oddly, however, Ardal O'Hanlon (who plays Dougal) seems to think that despite the caricatures that these characters humanised the church:

> 'I thought in some way it put a human face on the church. It humanised these people. You know, monstrous as some of them are, Father Jack is an outrageous creation, but it humanised them. Father Ted is so downtrodden, he's always so hard-pressed but he's a decent guy at the end of the day.'[11]

The church, though, takes something of a backseat in the programme. The church setting provides some of the comedy scenes, but as the series developed, the plots became increasingly more surreal, some based on popular films such as the episode 'Speed 3' – working on the premise that there couldn't be a worse sequel than the film *Speed 2* – which sees Dougal on an out of control milk float rigged with a bomb.[12] In fact, that episode is the only episode to feature the saying of mass – and that was for a very funny joke – the priests not having any other skills it is the only thing they can think of doing in response to the growing crisis situation:

Ted: Another Mass? That's our best idea?

Beeching: Well, I thought the other one went very well.

Ted: He needs help, not Mass! He needs physical lifting off the milkfloat, not spiritual lifting of his ... spirits. There's a time for Mass and a time for action. And this is a time for action! ...

Beeching: Is there *anything* to be said for saying another Mass …? Just a small one. God, I love saying Mass.[13]

On the whole, though, the writers stay away from the church and its practices and find the humour elsewhere – almost using the priests as a blank canvas to play with:

'One of the great things about priests is that they all dress the same. So you can take a concept, impose it on a priest and it becomes funny almost automatically.'[14]

In the series, some fun is had with some of the scandals of the church – such as in episodes like 'The Passion of St Tibulus', which lampoons how the church accidentally becomes chief marketing officer when a risqué film comes out: 'Down with this sort of thing. Careful now.'[15] That episode also features the blackmailing of Bishop Brennan after a video tape is found of him with his American son and mistress, frolicking on the beach in full bishop's regalia. Or in my personal favourite 'Kicking Bishop Brennan Up the Arse' Catholics are mocked for their obsession with finding the face of Jesus or other saints in everyday items. However, the church is not the main focus of the fun or the mockery, *Father Ted* is driven by its characters and this far eclipses any perceived 'attack on the church' intended or otherwise.

The sad thing is that the naivety and nostalgia of the programme belongs back in the 1990s when it was made. Since then, the many revelations of the terrible abuses carried out on children by priests hiding behind the protection of the institution have altered our view of the church forever. *Father Ted* simply could not be made now. Graham Linehan admitted as much in an interview:

> 'I was never beaten or abused by priests who taught me at CUS [Catholic University School, his secondary school in Dublin] – some of them were a bit eccentric but they all seemed harmless enough. But since Ted, and everything that's come out, I've just come to really hate the church. I could never write Ted now because I'd be so angry my fingers would go through the keyboard.'[16]

Silly, light-hearted, portrayals of priests now are thin on the ground on our television screens, and it's obvious why that is. Tom Doran wrote in a comment piece: 'What we now know places the Irish Church beyond the domain of comedy.'[17] The abuse scandals might also explain why the more recent portrayals of clergy in drama (such as in *Broadchurch* and *Rev.*) have been more fully rounded and realistic rather than caricatures. It is simply very difficult in the light of what we now know to make jokes about priests.

Ordinary Christians

All of the characters I have explored so far have been clergy. There are a number of reasons for this. Clergy represent a world that is quite mysterious to many outsiders; they have a lot of comedic potential because of the nature of what they do (dressing up in funny clothes, intoning funny words) and they are sometimes figures of authority that could do with taking down a peg or two. So what of the ordinary Christian? It is very rare to see a Christian character on television whose Christian faith is just part of who they are rather than something essential to the plot (such as in a crime drama). Although this book is largely about the British context, I could not write this without some reference to *The Simpsons*. *The Simpsons* is the only programme on television (that I can think of) that regularly portrays people of faith (Christian, Jewish, Hindu...) as ordinary, whose faith is part of their everyday lives. Creator Matt Groening said in an interview in 1999:

> 'Right-wingers complain there's no God on TV. Not only do the Simpsons go to church every Sunday and pray; they actually speak to God from time to time.'[18]

Granted, the cartoon features one of the greatest caricatures of a Christian ever in Homer's annoying neighbour Ned Flanders, but alongside that caricature is just the portrayal of ordinary people facing life's problems and turning to faith at certain points along the journey. Possibly, the fact that *The Simpsons* is a cartoon means that people are blinded to the sensitivity with which faith is portrayed in the programme. Perhaps it has a similar effect to *Father Ted* – in the placing of the action in a world that is parallel to ours but not the same we can discount it as 'not real' and therefore not reflective of real life. Add to that, the American mid-west setting and British people can say, 'Well, it's not like that here'. This is something of a shame, because the programme often deals with theological and spiritual themes. Former Archbishop of Canterbury Rowan Williams is a known fan and said of it that *The Simpsons* is 'generally on the side of the angels and on the side of sense. It punctures lots of pompous fictions about how the world works'.[19] It perhaps says something about our increasingly secularised culture that to find a genuine portrayal of a Christian on British television one has to look over the pond to an American cartoon.

# DOT BRANNING (NÉE COTTON)

Category: Good ☐ Bad ☐ Quirky ☑
Name: Dot Branning (née Cotton)
Actor: June Brown

Character details

Dot Branning has been a character in *EastEnders* since its inception in 1985. The chain-smoking, gossiping laundrette assistant on Albert Square has had her fair share of problems (as have all the characters in the soap opera) but often openly refers to her faith as what gets her through.

Score card:

Longevity	98%
Endearment	54%
Offence	58%
Vices	78%
Popularity	67%
Realism	82%

EastEnders

'You know me, I ain't one to gossip, but the word is…'

'I couldn't manage without my faith, not with the life I've had.'

There is one British television character who is a representation of an 'ordinary Christian', a lone figure in the expanse of television drama and comedy. She is the busybody woman many Christians love to hate: Dot Cotton (now Branning) from long-running BBC soap opera *EastEnders*. Dot is one of the few characters on British television who quotes the bible, speaks of her faith and her doubts and has theological questions. Here she speaks to her son about his father's death:

'Your father, he weren't a believer, and Sharon, she said to me that I could stop worrying about it on account of knowing where he is at last but I don't do I? ..."And fear not them which kill the body but are not able to kill the soul but rather fear him which can destroy both soul and body in hell" that's Matthew 10 verse 28. You see hell isn't fire and brimstone, it's being apart from God and if I am saved and he ain't then I shall be apart from him, unless he came to Jesus in the end...'

EastEnders is famous for tackling big issues and over the years Dot's character has been a touchstone for themes ranging from homophobia, euthanasia and cancer – these themes being looked at through the prism of Dot's fairly conservative faith. Although she's a great gossip, she is also known as a caring compassionate character who, at least for much of the time the programme has been on air, is generally forgiving of her criminal son Nick's behaviour. There seems to be a difference of opinion over the authenticity of her character between those who are Christians and those who are not. Many Christians despise her character, largely because she is the only Christian character on television and is often depicted representing the more reactionary side of the church. Those who are not believers like her, because she confirms their own prejudices about Christians and, because of her age, can dismiss her (and by extension the church) as old and irrelevant.

In 2002 the former executive producer of *EastEnders* spoke to an audience of clergy in the diocese of St Albans defending the soap as being a force for moral good. He referred to the famous euthanasia storyline where Dot was asked by her friend to help her die:

The 'quirky'

'Dot – the character the *Mail on Sunday* claimed we made fun of – explored the full panoply of religious belief before coming back to terms with her maker.

As she said to her vicar towards the end of the story, in my favourite line of *EastEnders'* entire existence, "I couldn't manage without my faith, not with the life I've had".

When Alan Bookbinder took over as head of religious broadcasting at the BBC he described *EastEnders* for the weeks the Dot and Ethel story ran as "the best religious programme on television" and compared us to Graham Greene.'[20]

There aren't many dramas on television that are brave enough to explore big theological and moral questions that are the stuff of everyday life. We might get crime dramas and documentaries covering such issues, but to see them covered in the minutiae of daily life is something that *EastEnders* is actually quite good at.

No matter whether you feel that *EastEnders* is reflective or not of our culture, the character of Dot does seem to have some internal consistency. The actress who plays her recently confessed that she had occasionally changed Dot's lines to make them more consistent with her own Christian beliefs:

'I think I've made Dot more like me, it's something I've done which I don't approve of because I think you should play characters like they're written but they don't always write the prayers and the behaviour for a Christian into it. And I'm afraid that I have changed it. Her faith and my faith has changed her.'[21]

So as far as the actress June Brown is concerned Dot's faith is quite real. Even in the dramatic events of the thirtieth anniversary episodes in 2015 where Dot is accused of letting her drug-taking son die 'so that he wouldn't hurt any more people', her faith is at the centre of her responses. When sitting with Nick who has taken an overdose she tells him:

> 'I ain't called the ambulance, I prayed to let Jesus decide whether you get better or whether the world was a better place without you.'
>
> Nick responds: 'I'm sorry, ma. For everything I ever put you through. Forgive me.'
>
> 'Confess to Jesus, he'll forgive you,' she replies.[22]

It seems the writers cannot separate Dot's faith from her character – and in some ways that is to be applauded as it recognises that faith is not an add-on or a hobby, but integral to people's lives.

The issue, of course, is the expectation that a single character in a soap opera can be representative of all people of a very diverse faith. She simply can't bear that burden, even though television executives have tried to make her do that. When challenged that people of faith are depicted on BBC television as 'freaks, geeks or antiques', Danny Cohen (then Controller of BBC One) presented Dot Branning as 'a single example of someone who lives out her faith on television in a charitable way.'[23] This was met with some disdain by Christians at the event at which he was speaking. Revd Hayley Matthews, chaplain for MediaCity UK (BBC North's base in Salford) said: 'I don't think Dot Cotton is very representative of

Christians. I think a lot of people would be offended by that.' Matthew Adcock, from the London School of Theology, admitted that although Dot was portrayed as a Christian she did not represent the country's 'growing, younger demographic'.[24]

Dot Branning *is* an example of a certain type of Christian on our televisions; the problem is that she is the *only* one. Challenged to think of a Christian on television who was not a 'freak, geek or antique', the only person Cohen could think of was Dot Branning – he was clutching at straws, as, at the age of 87, Dot could be referred to as something of an antique. This is, unfortunately, the view of the church and Christians in secular culture and, if we are honest, does represent something of the demographics of Church of England today, with the average age of a church attender being 61.[25]

There are a number of reasons, I think, why we don't see many 'ordinary' Christian characters on our televisions. First, religion is not something that is particularly public in British culture. In America it is fine to state proudly 'in God we trust' but in Britain even some Christians cringe at such bold statements. Anthropologist Kate Fox describes this well: 'Earnestness of any kind makes us squirm. Religious earnestness makes us deeply suspicious and decidedly twitchy.'[26] Second, Christianity is a diverse faith. One only has to look (actually, don't) at the recent debates of the Church of England's General Synod around women bishops and gay marriage to realise that we do not all believe exactly the same things. It would be impossible for just a few characters even to represent the breadth of beliefs in modern Britain: for one character with whom you identified there would

be four others you did not. Third, the quiet faith lived
by the ordinary Christian is not the stuff of television
drama or comedy: it's not that interesting, it's neither
sensational nor funny. Where we do see it, in something
such as *EastEnders* through Dot Branning's character, it
is more often in relation to a moral issue the story is
covering, rather than because it is part of the character's
life. Television writers write to entertain; and although
truth-telling is a big part of what they do, they also need
to keep people engaged and interested.

Let's think, though, would it ever be possible to get
a decent representation of Christians on television? I'm
sure your view of what would be a good representation
would be very different from mine. I don't want to sit and
watch a series of characters who are 'just like me'. It is far
better to have representations that challenge us and that
we can use as a springboard to discussing faith.

Rowan Atkinson – rent-a-vicar

In the 1960s and 1970s the go-to man for playing clerics
on screen was the plummy voiced Derek Nimmo in
programmes like *All Gas and Gaiters*, *Oh Brother!* and *Hell's
Bells*. Nimmo's portrayals of bumbling clerics, although
now largely forgotten, can still be heard a little in the
vicar characters of today. Nimmo's characterisations
are seared in the popular imagination: as I watched
episodes of *All Gas and Gaiters* in researching this book
I completely recognised the clergy stereotype even
though I had never watched it before. In more recent
years there has not been a more prolific actor than
Rowan Atkinson (*Blackadder*, *Mr Bean*) at playing Church

of England vicars. Many of the vicar characters played by Atkinson are the fruit of his partnership with writer Richard Curtis. Where Curtis' Vicar of Dibley, Geraldine Granger, set out to challenge the *All Gas and Gaiters*-style aloof, upper-class clergy stereotype, Rowan Atkinson steals shamelessly from it.

Atkinson has played at least ten different vicar characters since about 1981, clearly finding the role a source of comedy and inspiration – possibly informed by his experiences as a youngster at Durham Chorister School. In radical 1980s comedy sketch show *Not the Nine O'Clock News* he was in four sketches as a vicar character. The first is a hilarious imagining of a vicar's experience of the BBC coming to film *Songs of Praise* in his small, sleepy parish:

> 'Last week, the congregation numbered seven. Four of whom had turned up a week early by mistake. And the week before that, Harvest Sunday, there were three of us: myself, the organist (Mr Posner) and a tin of spaghetti [shouting] WHERE WERE YOU BASTARDS THEN?
>
> …Christ was right wasn't he? When two or three are gathered in my name the service can't be on television!'

This appearance was largely inoffensive (perhaps with the exception of the bad language) and the joke is more on the hypocrisy of church attenders than on the clergy themselves. There is even a clear biblical reference (Matthew 18:20) as he misquotes Jesus 'When two or three are gathered…' betraying a childhood spent in church.

Another sketch involves a vicar character being in a debate about the proliferation of bad language on television

– this sketch is funny because each character in the debate accidentally drops 'rude' words into everything they say – again, this is largely inoffensive as the joke is about the play on words rather than directed at the clergy or beliefs per se.

A final sketch in the same programme is much more offensive. It depicts a young vicar trying to be trendy asking the question 'are you a gay Christian?' and struggling to get his terminology right: 'Don't be ashamed! Stand up! Come out of the toilet, as the phrase has it' and ending with the very sad line, which reveals Atkinson's own opinion of the church as homophobic: 'God just wants you to have a rotten life. He's like that. He hates poofs.'

Atkinson performed three vicar sketches in his live shows. Some of these are more offensive than others. One involves a sermon at a wedding:

> 'A lot of prospective brides ask me these days, Father, what is the church's attitude to fellatio? And I tend to reply by telling them a little story about the first time I was asked that question. It was a couple of years ago now and a young attractive bride-to-be came up to me after a service and asked me just that question: "Father, what is the church's attitude to fellatio?" And I replied, "Well, you know, Joanne, I'd *like* to tell you but unfortunately I don't know what fellatio is" and so she showed me. And ever since, whenever anyone has asked me the question "Father, what is the church's attitude to fellatio?" I always reply "Well, I'd *like* to tell you but unfortunately I don't know what fellatio is." '

Part of the humour in this sketch is derived from the idea of a vicar both speaking openly about an intimate sex act. Some might find that offensive – although I didn't. What I *did* find offensive in watching this sketch, is that throughout – perhaps in a bid to make the vicar character appear very laid-back – Atkinson is casually eating a communion wafer, pausing to dip it in a chalice as if it is a bar snack. Curiously, I found that quite strongly offensive – where I suspect Atkinson himself would assume that I would be more offended by the topic of sex. This shows a similar ignorance to that which I explored earlier on the part of comedy show *Goodness Gracious Me* and their communion sketch. What Atkinson has failed to understand is the significance of the symbols of communion, and has appropriated them for a sketch perhaps unknowingly causing offence.

In another sketch in his live show, there is a spoof gospel reading by a priest of the story of the Wedding at Cana, where Jesus turns the water into wine:

'...and when the steward of the feast did taste of the water from the pots, it had become wine, and they knew not whence it had come. But the servants did know, and they applauded loudly in the kitchen, and they said unto the Lord, "How the hell did you do that?" and enquired of him "Do you do children's parties?" '

To a degree, this sketch depends on the audience having heard a reading in church before and actually knowing the story of the miracle at Cana. There is a subtle atheist jibe that Jesus' miracles were nothing more than parlour tricks but it is an amusing spoof of the language of the King James Bible and at least, in a similar manner to Eddie Izzard's comedy, actually engages with a real bit of scripture. One wonders whether this sketch would still produce the similar peals of laughter that it originally did in the 1980s with an audience of under-25 year olds today.

Another sketch centres around a film entitled 'Life of Python' – a funny spoof of the reaction to *Monty Python's Life of Brian*. In this parody, Rowan Atkinson plays a bishop who has directed this 'blasphemous' film against Pythonians. The bishop character is a thinly veiled caricature of Bishop Mervyn Stockwood who appeared on *Saturday Night, Sunday Morning* in 1979 and critiqued *Life of Brian*.

The last classic vicar sketch in his live show is the funeral sermon about the deaths of Tom, Dick and Harry. Atkinson is essentially telling a funny joke in the guise of a priest delivering a funeral address for three friends, Tom, Dick and Harry – Tom being blind, Dick deaf and Harry unable to speak, the address ends with the punchline:

> 'For Dick will see the angels' choir, Harry will hear the angels' choir, and no doubt Tom will ruin it for everybody.'

In this sketch, the vicar character and funeral setting are simply the delivery mechanism for a very funny joke and therefore secondary in importance.

So far these sketches reveal that there are a number of reasons Rowan Atkinson likes to play vicars: they are a good source of comedy, they work as an effective vehicle for a joke and they are an opportunity to challenge the church on its teaching. Let's look in a bit more detail at the three most recent vicar characters played by Atkinson – these are his best known and therefore most influential.

 **FATHER GERALD**

Category: Good ☐ Bad ☐ Quirky ☑
Name: Father Gerald
Actor: Rowan Atkinson

Character details

Father Gerald is the incredibly nervous vicar conducting his first wedding in 1990s blockbuster film *Four Weddings and a Funeral* directed by Richard Curtis. Rowan Atkinson plays the bumbling vicar to brilliant effect in one of the classic scenes of the film, fumbling his lines and mispronouncing the couples' names much to the delight of the on-screen (and off-screen) congregation.

Score card:

Longevity	81%
Endearment	78%
Offence	5%
Vices	10%
Popularity	90%
Realism	63%

Four Weddings and a Funeral

'In the name of the father, the son, and the holy spigot. Spirit!'

— Father Gerald (Rowan Atkinson) in
Four Weddings and a Funeral

Rowan Atkinson's bumbling priest in the British film *Four Weddings and a Funeral* (1994) is perhaps the ultimate stereotype of the male Church of England vicar. In the first wedding of the four featured in the film, Rowan Atkinson's Father Gerald is taking a wedding for the first time, visibly uncomfortable in his rich vestments and biretta (black priest's hat). Right from his introductory 'In the name of the Father, and the Son and the Holy Spirit' we can feel

his nerves, plunging both the on-screen and off-screen congregation into a pique of anxiety. Richard Curtis captures the moment that many of us have experienced when a person leading a service is having an excruciating time, making lots of mistakes and the congregation are doing their best to either stifle giggles or urge the vicar to get through it. There is nothing, I would contend, funnier than getting the giggles in a context in which it is inappropriate to laugh. This happened to me a few years ago when visiting a church with my husband. My husband was brought up in a rugby playing family – as a child he used to listen to his father's records of rugby songs with the rude words bleeped out. Some of these songs we have since begun to sing with gusto on long car journeys. One in particular that was passed on to me is the pretty filthy 'The Mayor of Bayswater's Daughter' sung to the Welsh folk tune 'The Ash Grove'. We turned up at the church, slightly conspicuous as an unusually young couple on a Sunday morning (hence attracting some attention) and we came to sing the Gloria. Yes, you've guessed it, the tune for this hymn of praise was 'The Ash Grove'. The giggles began to bubble up as we tried to sing sacred words to what in our mind was a profane tune. My husband had to sit down and put his head in his hands in a posture of deep piety to hide the hilarity. I held my order of service in front of my face and it shook violently as I tried to stifle the laughter. I have never laughed so much. Experiences like this are what Richard Curtis is tapping with this scene in *Four Weddings and a Funeral*.

Unlike some of his other vicar characters, this one is largely sympathetic rather than cuttingly satirical. As Father Gerald finally gets to the end of the ceremony, Simon

Callow's character Gareth bellows (a rather patronising – but deservedly so) 'BRAVO!' and leads the congregation in clapping not the newly-weds but the vicar for getting through it.

When it was released in 1994 *Four Weddings and a Funeral* was perhaps the greatest British export for years. It came out at a time when British movies and music were deeply unfashionable. It presented a picture of modern Britain which played into stereotypes focusing on London, country villages, lovely churches and the upper classes (things of fascination to the Americans) and as a result heralded the beginning of 'Cool Britannia' – the resurgence of confidence in Britishness reflected in Britpop music and exploited by the New Labour government. Again, as we saw earlier, the church is at the centre of a nostalgic portrayal of England. Awkwardness of communication is a theme of the film and a characteristically British trait. Father Gerald is hilariously awkward where Hugh Grant's character Charles is endearingly awkward – his floppy-haired stuttering declarations of love became the actor's trademark.

Rowan Atkinson is a master of physical comedy and verbal dexterity. He is wonderful at speech impediments and mispronunciations probably because he has a mild stammer himself. Perhaps the reason Atkinson is the go-to actor for the role of vicar is because there are very few other public roles that have such comedic potential. After all, vicars are dressed in funny clothes (which are also a trip hazard), they have to recite arcane religious words in front of large groups of bemused people while juggling books and papers, they have to remember to get the names of the people they are marrying, burying or christening correct: the slapstick potential is endless.

The 'quirky'

Put this into the context of a serious church service and there is every expectation of hilarity. Kate Fox says in *Watching the English* that:

> 'We have an intense need for the rules and formalities of ritual, but at the same time we find these ceremonies acutely embarrassing and uncomfortable.'[27]

All of this comes together perfectly in the character of Father Gerald in the opening wedding of the film, playing up to all our expectations and creating a characteristically British cringefest which unfortunately is all too familiar.

Father Gerald is pure stereotype and represents the apex of Rowan Atkinson's portrayals of vicars – nervous, bumbling, embarrassing and posh.

REVD WALTER GOODFELLOW

Category: Good ☐   Bad ☐   Quirky ☑
Name: Dot Branning (née Cotton)
Actor: June Brown

Character details

Revd Walter Goodfellow is the protagonist of 2005 film *Keeping Mum*. He is the vicar of sleepy village Little Wallop, struggling to keep his marriage going and trying to write a sermon for a big clergy conference when a mysterious Mary Poppins-like figure comes into their lives. And people start to go missing.

Score card:

Longevity	61%
Endearment	68%
Offence	10%
Vices	13%
Popularity	74%
Realism	89%

Keeping Mum

'The title for this evening's opening address is Cod's
Mysterious Ways. God! God! God's Mysterious Ways'
— Revd Walter Goodfellow (Rowan Atkinson)
in *Keeping Mum*

The Revd Walter Goodfellow is an altogether different
beast from Father Gerald in *Four Weddings* although the
two characters do share some DNA. Walter is more
of a straight role for Rowan Atkinson in 2005 British
comedy drama *Keeping Mum*. Atkinson says in a 'making
of' featurette: 'It was a comedy of a much greater subtlety
than I am usually associated with'.[28] To an extent, Walter is
an everyman character who happens also to be a priest,
Atkinson confesses: 'I've played a number of vicars in my
time but that was not the thing that drew me to it, indeed
arguably it might have been something that put me off!' In
this film, the vicar character is chosen to add to the cosy
English scenes conjured up. Yet again the English village with
its church at the centre is exploited for effect – in this
film to expose the darker undercurrents of idyllic country
life: 'I had precise views about the look of the film but the
overriding principle was this idea of sweet, normal England
and what happens under the surface' says director Niall
Johnson.[29]

Revd Walter is a man whose priorities have all become
skewed to the point at which he is both neglecting his
family and simultaneously failing in his role as parish priest,
Atkinson explains: 'He's someone blinded by his own

curiosity about the meaning of life and the nature of life and therefore he's blinded to the problems that he has in his own family.'[30] Walter and his family are saved by a Mary Poppins-type figure played by Maggie Smith who has some big secrets of her own.

Keeping Mum is like *Four Weddings* in that it exploits the nostalgic English scene of a village to explore themes of relationships. There is also a little of Father Gerald in Revd Walter as Walter trips over his words in his address at a big clergy conference at the climax of the film:

> 'The title for this evening's opening address is Cod's Mysterious Ways. God! God! God's Mysterious Ways'.

The 'quirky'

The stereotype dial for this vicar character, however, is set on 'mild', as is the satire. Atkinson comments that 'Walter is a very decent man and I've not played many decent men.'[31] The character in this film is a vicar not because vicars are inherently funny (as in *Four Weddings*) but to support the storyline which focuses on faith, crime and grace (not accidentally the name of Maggie Smith's character). Surely, however, the years of playing clergy characters meant that Rowan Atkinson could slip into the dog collar with ease, knowing just how to fumble with papers at a lectern for comedic effect.

THE ARCHBISHOP OF CANTERBURY

Category: Good ☐ Bad ☐ Quirky ☑
Name: The Archbishop of Canterbury
Actor: Rowan Atkinson

Character details

For the popular charity fundraiser, Comic Relief, in 2013, Rowan Atkinson created a sketch in which he played the 'new' Archbishop of Canterbury. He presents the character as an old establishment figure trying to come across as 'in touch' with popular culture by trying to encourage people to give to Comic Relief while mentioning a few 'rude words' and talking about what a tremendous sense of humour God has.

Score card:

Longevity	15%
Endearment	2%
Offence	81%
Vices	24%
Popularity	51%
Realism	9%

Comic Relief

> 'It's my job to remind you of the spiritual nature of a night like this. Jesus said "love your neighbour" and let's be perfectly clear because there's a lot of misunderstanding about this, he didn't say "shag your neighbour".'
>
> — Rowan Atkinson as The Archbishop of Canterbury in a sketch for Comic Relief 2013

Rowan Atkinson's most recent clergy character was his depiction of the new Archbishop of Canterbury sharing his message for Comic Relief in 2013 (Justin Welby having become the new Archbishop in the January of that year). Here are some quotes from the sketch:

> 'It's my job to remind you of the spiritual nature of a night like this. Jesus said "love your neighbour" and let's be perfectly clear because there's a lot of misunderstanding about this, he didn't say "shag your neighbour".'
>
> 'In a way, when what you think you're doing is watching One Direction singing their fabulous new sound (I love One Direction, and so does Jesus, they remind him of the disciples) what you're actually watching is Christianity in action.'
>
> 'For now, from all of us at the good old C of E, have a wonderful night, keep on giving, keep on laughing, keep on praying (it doesn't work but it's a good part of a getting to sleep campaign if you've got insomnia).'[32]

This sketch, which was presented as the Archbishop's message in support of giving money to Comic Relief (something that most Christians would support), was the most complained about broadcast of 2013 with 2,200 complaints (although only a quarter of these complaints were regarding 'religious' content, the rest being about inappropriate language before the watershed).[33] I wanted to complain about this sketch as well, but it was not because of the quip that 'prayer doesn't work' or the mention of 'shagging'. I wanted to complain because given Atkinson's previously excellent form at playing clerics, it simply was not funny.

Earlier, I explored what works and doesn't work with humour about religion. One theme that came through was the importance of the satire reflecting reality – it needs that

'aha' moment. This Archbishop character was recognisable but only as a relic of the past rather than as a reflection of clergy today.

Justin Welby was quite a surprise appointment to Canterbury – having worked in the oil industry before coming to ordination later in life, rarely wearing a purple shirt and able to parry with journalists with much greater ease than his predecessor, the rather more academic and wizard-like Rowan Williams. It has been literally years since a bishop has 'addressed the nation' in a genial manner akin to the set-up for this sketch. The last time a bishop was given lots of airtime like that was perhaps the Bishop of Southwark when he appeared in his purple cassock on the ill-fated episode of *Saturday Night, Sunday Morning* during which he lambasted the new Monty Python film *Life of Brian* in 1979. In the original debate Mervyn Stockwood fiddles throughout with his pectoral cross and keeps taking his specs on and off. Later in the debate he wags his finger a lot at Michael Palin and treats him like a naughty school boy. It is this kind of upper class, imperious cleric that Rowan Atkinson is having a go at. Atkinson had already played a bishop before – mercilessly mimicking Mervyn Stockwood in the sketch 'Life of Python' – this is the image of a bishop that Atkinson had in mind for this Comic Relief sketch – he just, ironically, happens to be 35 years too late!

I suspect that this dislike of a particular kind of cleric had been building up in Rowan Atkinson. In an interview in *The Times* in 2011 he stated:

'I used to think that the vicars that I played [and he has played a lot of them, even in his straight roles] or the exaggerated sketches that were written about clerics, were unreasonable satires on well-meaning individuals but, actually, so many of the clerics that I've met, particularly the Church of England clerics, are people of such extraordinary smugness and arrogance and conceitedness who are extraordinarily presumptuous about the significance of their position in society. Increasingly, I believe that all the mud that Richard Curtis and I threw at them through endless sketches that we've done is more than deserved.'[34]

Read, for that, 'no more Mr Nice Guy' – and two years later we get this unfunny spoof of an out of touch bishop. I am happy for pomposity and abuse of power to be subjected to satire – that's the great thing about the comedy tradition of this country. I have enjoyed many of Rowan Atkinson's characterisations over the years and many of the criticisms that are behind some of the jokes are things that the church has needed to hear. The mud that was slung with this Comic Relief sketch, however, didn't hit its target.

What is going on here?

Society as we know it is changing at break-neck speed. The Church of England is changing at snail's pace, but it is changing. The clergy have become more professionalised with training for curates much more closely monitored than it ever was and all clergy expected to engage in continuing ministerial education and reflective practice – slowly catching up with the management techniques of the secular world. What this means is that it is becoming less and less likely that one would experience a bumbling vicar stereotype in church who would fumble their way through a service mispronouncing people's names. The truth is that those embarrassing, incompetent vicar-types are literally dying out. It seems as though they are dying out on our television screens as well.

The lack of ordinary Christian characters on television perpetuates the pervading view that the church is in serious decline and has less and less influence in our society. Christians are in enough of a minority now to not warrant too much airtime, resulting in those of religious faith complaining that the religious are usually portrayed on television as 'freaks, geeks or antiques'. The thing is, freaks, geeks and antiques are entertaining and religious groups have more than their fair share. Take a look around your local church congregation and you'll find plenty of them. Perhaps we should fly the flag of our oddness a little more. What we have seen in looking at these 'quirky' characters is a tour of the current state of our culture and its attitude to religion. We can see, depicted in these characters, the decline of the church's position in society, the view that the religious are a bit bonkers and the idea that the church is both out of date and irrelevant. This is simply where we are.

Our response

Is it uniquely people of faith, though, who are unfairly portrayed? What about the police, or nurses or teachers? We have to admit, I think, that some pleasure can be taken in the feeling that one is in a persecuted minority (a minority that has food on the table and a roof over its head, a good job and a loving healthy family). In the grand scheme of things it does not really amount to persecution if a character on television is not quite the kind of Christian character you would like to see. It probably does reflect our secular society quite truthfully, and we have to come to terms with that. Pope Benedict XVI described Christians as needing to see themselves now as a 'creative minority':

> 'In times of liminality, such as the one that the West is presently passing through, it is more important to live as creative minorities than to live either as coercive minorities or as ineffective majorities.'[35]

Like it or not, Christendom no longer exists. A programme like *All Gas and Gaiters* about the machinations at the top of the church could no longer be made. That cultural knowledge is now gone and the church has certainly lost its position of authority – which is not necessarily a bad thing. Necessity is the mother of invention – we can be creative about the fact that there are not so many Christians being portrayed on television. We can laugh along with the stereotypes and gentle mocking of authority figures and challenge, if we like, the things that don't feel accurate. I'd certainly rather be in a creative than a coercive minority – it's much more fun for a start.

What would Jesus watch?

**'It is a test of a good religion whether
you can joke about it.'**
— G.K. Chesterton

What are we to do with all this?

In Britain we have a very rich comedy heritage, one of our outstanding characteristics as a nation is our famed sense of humour (which many don't quite understand). It is part of the bedrock of who we are:

'there may indeed be something distinctive about English humour, the real "defining characteristic" is the *value* we put on humour, the central importance of humour in English culture and social interactions. In other cultures, there is "a time and a place" for humour; it is a special, separate kind of talk. In English conversation, there is always an undercurrent of humour. We can barely manage to say "hello" or comment on the weather without somehow contriving to make a bit of a joke out of it, and most English conversations will involve at least some degree of banter, teasing, irony, understatement, humorous self-deprecation, mockery or just silliness. Humour is our "default mode".[1]

I would suggest that we would not have this rich use of comedy in our culture if we were not informed by Judaeo-Christian thinking. Believe it or not, in its original form, Christianity was an incredibly radical religion. It is a religion founded on the challenge of misuse of power – something for which humour has been used throughout history.

In the 1990s I had a cheesy wristband that had the initials 'W.W.J.D.' – these stood for What Would Jesus Do? The idea of the bracelet was to act as a reminder to try and imitate Christ in all situations. A noble aim to be sure. Australian comedy band Axis of Awesome did, however, point out a slight flaw in the logic in their 'What Would Jesus Do?' song. The song imagines the scenario of being at a party when the wine runs out, you think 'What Would Jesus Do?' and realise, oh, 'He's a million, billion, trillion times better than you'. Fair point guys! However, I would like to suggest we bring WWJD back when we're watching telly. What would Jesus do in response to *Father Ted* or *Rev.*? Would he laugh? I'd like to think that he probably would, and here I present my evidence:

5 ways Jesus Christ gives modern stand-ups a run for their money

1. Being offensive

Jesus knew all about how to offend people and used it to great effect. Nearly all of his offensive comments are against not 'the sinners' as one might expect, given the way people have preached fire and brimstone over the years, but against the religious leaders of his day – the Pharisees who placed intolerable burdens on the people:

> 'Woe to you, scribes and Pharisees, hypocrites! For you are like whitewashed tombs, which on the outside look beautiful, but inside they are full of the bones of the dead and of all kinds of filth. So you also on the outside look righteous to others, but inside you are full of hypocrisy and lawlessness.'
> Matthew 23: 27–8

There is a whole list of insults in Matthew chapter 23, it goes on and on and even to the untrained eye it is obvious that Jesus doesn't think much of these so-called religious teachers. Jesus' statements are so incendiary that the disciples have to take him to one side to tell him he is being too rude: 'Then the disciples approached and said to him, "Do you know that the Pharisees took offence when they heard what you said?" ' Matthew 15:11

2. Telling funny jokes

Jesus uses hyperbole almost as much as Simon Cowell does on the *X Factor*. He regularly used ridiculous images to get his point across – and also, to get a laugh! Where? Well he describes the mustard bush as the 'largest of all trees' (which even we in the modern world know is patently not true, but it was a long time before I realised that Jesus is being intentionally funny). He says that it is harder for a camel to go through the eye of a needle than a rich man to enter the kingdom of heaven. For centuries people have tried to figure out what he meant, where, in reality, he was describing something amusingly impossible to say simply that – it's impossible for a rich man to enter the kingdom of heaven. It's a comic image to put across a point, not anything more complex than that. Gerald Arbuckle says: 'In first century Palestine people would have most likely laughed at many of Jesus's intentionally ridiculous illustrations, for example, the idea that someone would have lit a lamp and put it under a basket, or that a person would have built a house on sand, or that a father would give a child stones instead of bread.'[2] We miss most of this because, as Revd Daniel J. Herrington, an expert on the New Testament says: 'Humour is very culture-bound. The Gospels have a lot of controversy stories and honour-shame situations. I suspect that the early readers found these stories hilarious, whereas we in a very different social setting miss the point entirely.'[3]

There we are: Jesus was hilarious.

3. Giving nicknames to his mates

Jesus had a self-picked gang of friends in the disciples. As in any group of friends, he gave some of them nicknames – most famously, of course, Peter whose original name was Simon. Peter means 'rock' (after Jesus names him he goes on to say that Peter will be the 'rock' on which he builds his church). The more I read of the gospels the more I think this was probably quite an ironic nickname. Peter is the one who always jumps in (sometimes literally – see Matthew 14:29 and John 21:7) with two feet. He's reliable, but not in a good way – you can rely on Peter to get it wrong. Not a rock-like quality. It's testimony to both Jesus' sense of humour and also his faith that Peter would make it in the end (even after denying him three times) that he gives him this nickname. An encouragement to us all!

Jesus also nicknames the brothers James and John (sons of Zebedee – no, not that Zebedee) the Sons of Thunder. The mind boggles as to this one, but I guess they argued a lot or maybe they were just really loud, or maybe Jesus is even referring in this epithet to their pushy mother? Then, some of the others also had nicknames. There's another Simon – but that one is nicknamed the Zealot (that could probably be translated as terrorist today) and poor Thomas (as in doubting) is simply known by most of his friends as 'the twin' (Didymus in Greek) – which any identical twin could sympathise with. When I list the nicknames like this you can almost hear the banter amongst these young men.

4. Sticking it to 'the man'

Some of the most controversial comedians of the last few years have been famous for challenging the government and other authority figures – Alexei Sayle, Ben Elton (in the 1980s), Bill Hicks, Tim Minchin, Mark Thomas… Jesus gives these guys a run for their money too. He shockingly describes Herod, the puppet ruler of the Jews, as a fox:

> At that very hour some Pharisees came and said to him, 'Get away from here, for Herod wants to kill you.' He said to them, 'Go and tell that

fox for me, "Listen, I am casting out demons and performing cures today and tomorrow, and on the third day I finish my work. Yet today, tomorrow, and the next day I must be on my way, because it is impossible for a prophet to be killed away from Jerusalem." ' (Luke 13:31–3)

It is, ultimately, what leads to his death, directly challenging the religious authorities of his day that they've got it wrong about God – and then being executed by the pagan Roman authorities for stirring up dissent. You can't get much more 'sticking it to the man' than that.

5. Being satirical

Not only did Jesus offend the sensibilities of the religious leaders and insult the politicians, he also engaged in powerful satirical acts, most clearly in his 'triumphal entry' into Jerusalem. The Romans were big fans of triumphal entries – soldiers would return from battle in a grand procession of war horses, weapons and chariots – perhaps headed by Caesar himself or a local ruler – into the city. It was a show of strength, a show of the dominance of *Pax Romana* – the 'peace of Rome' – a way to keep the people in fear of those who ruled them. Around the time of Passover, in Jerusalem, Pontius Pilate (the Roman leader) probably would have arranged just such a triumphal entry to assert Roman authority at a time when the city would be full of pilgrims celebrating their most important festival. And what does Jesus do? He conducts his own 'triumphal entry' but not on a war horse, on a baby donkey, a colt. This is a challenging satirical act. The people shout out praise to Jesus, as they might have been paid to do to the Romans. They lay down palm branches. Perhaps the reason the crowds were so supportive of this act of Jesus was because they could see how satirical it was – they wanted to join in this mockery of Roman authority. You can infer this because the Pharisees tell Jesus to stop the people shouting out for fear of Roman reprisals (Luke 19:40). There is something of the political cartoon or spoof YouTube video about Jesus' 'triumphal entry'. It seems, then, that Jesus was also a satirist.

So next time you're watching a stand-up comedian, and you have a sharp intake of breath at a comment about a politician or religious leader – think how those early multitudes might have responded in a similar way to Jesus and realise that they're only copying the Master.

Epilogue

'Humour seems almost a prerequisite for sanctity'
— James Martin, SJ[1]

Where's our wonder, our sense of humour when approaching the things of God? Why do so many people think that we have to leave our personalities behind when we go to church or read the bible? Can we learn to laugh at ourselves and realise that religion, although a serious part of life can also be a source of humour or even entertainment?

Emo Phillips puts this better than me in his classic joke:

Once I saw this guy on a bridge about to jump. I said, 'Don't do it!' He said, 'Nobody loves me.' I said, 'God loves you. Do you believe in God?'

He said, 'Yes.' I said, 'Are you a Christian or a Jew?' He said, 'A Christian.' I said, 'Me, too! Protestant or Catholic?' He said, 'Protestant.' I said, 'Me, too! What franchise?' He said, 'Baptist.' I said, 'Me, too! Northern Baptist or Southern Baptist?' He said, 'Northern Baptist.' I said, 'Me, too! Northern Conservative Baptist or Northern Liberal Baptist?'

He said, 'Northern Conservative Baptist.' I said, 'Me, too! Northern Conservative Baptist Great Lakes Region, or Northern Conservative Baptist Eastern Region?' He said, 'Northern Conservative Baptist Great Lakes Region.' I said, 'Me, too! Northern Conservative Baptist Great Lakes Region Council of 1879, or Northern Conservative Baptist Great Lakes Region Council of 1912?' He said, 'Northern Conservative Baptist Great Lakes Region Council of 1912.' I said, 'Die, heretic!' And I pushed him over.[2]

James Martin says: 'Humour seems almost a prerequisite for sanctity. The saints knew to take the long view of things, were quick to laugh at life's absurdities (and themselves), and always placed their trust in God.'[3] How reassuring to think that we can be saintly when we laugh at ourselves!

I hope in this tour of the good, the bad and the quirky of Christians on television we've seen just that – the full gamut of human life, the noble and ignoble, the hilarious and the downright embarrassing; that it has said something about our British culture – our love of self-deprecation and the unique church–state set up that we have; that it has also said something about how our society is changing, people are, interestingly, becoming curious about people of faith – because we are in more of a minority.

So, before you climb up onto your soapbox to ride your high horse, when you next see a Christian character on television think: What would Jesus do? And remember, when answering that question, freaking out and flipping tables is a viable option! Other possible actions you could

Epilogue

take include: taking the plank out of your own eye; thanking the Lord you're nothing like that; considering the lilies of the field; or writing a strongly worded letter to *Points of View*.

Notes

Preface

1   Olly Grant, 'From Sanctity to Sleuthing', *Church Times*, 19 September 2014.
2   A question asked of Danny Cohen, BBC One Controller at the Church and Media Conference in 2013.

Introduction

1   Eddie Izzard quoted in '*Life of Brian*: Comedy or Blasphemy?' Ship of Fools website, 1999 http://old.shipoffools.com/Cargo/Features99/Features/Brian.html.
2   My thanks to James Cary for introducing me to the Bechdel test – and for writing a sitcom in *Bluestone 42* that passes said test!
3   'Development of a BBC Diversity Strategy Summary of Responses to Public and Staff Consultations', *Public Knowledge*, 31 January 2011.

The 'good'

1   'Dawn French nearly turned down Vicar of Dibley', *BBC News Entertainment and the Arts*, 23 December 2012.
2   Bill Bryson, *Notes from a Small Island*, London, HarperCollins, 1997.
3   Blur, 'Bank Holiday', *Parklife* album, 1994.

4   Elizabeth F. Loftus, 'Illusions of memory', *Proceedings of the American Philosophical Society,* Vol. 142, No. 1, March 1998, pp. 60–73.

5   Kate Hilpern, 'Is your mind playing tricks on you?', *Guardian*, 16 September 2008

6   Tim Wildshut *et al.*, 'Nostalgia: Content, triggers, functions', *Journal of Personality and Social Psychology,* Vol. 91, No. 5, 2006, pp. 975–93.

7   *That Mitchell and Webb Look*, Series 3, BBC DVD, 2009.

8   Eddie Izzard, *Dress to Kill*, 1998

9   Kate Fox, *Watching the English*, London, Hodder & Stoughton, 2004, p. 354.

10   Quoted by Kate Fox in *Watching the English*, London: Hodder & Stoughton, 2004, p. 354.

11   Olly Grant, 'Clued up confessor on the box' *Church Times*, 11 January 2013.

12   Richard Curtis speaking in a documentary by Stuart Maconie, *The Real Vicars of Dibley*, BBC, 2002.

13   Richard Curtis speaking in a documentary by Stuart Maconie, *The Real Vicars of Dibley* BBC, 2002.

14   'The Vicar of Dibley Comic Relief Special', BBC, 2015.

15   (This quotation is often misattributed to William Booth.) George Whitefield, *The Monthly Review, or, Literary Journal,* Vol. 49, June 1773–January 1774, p. 430.

16   Stuart Maconie, *The Real Vicars of Dibley*, BBC, 2002

17   Kate Fox, *Watching the English*, London, Hodder & Stoughton, 2004.

18   David Herman, 'Horlicks for Chummy: Britain's romance with cosy TV nostalgia', *New Statesman*, 27 February 2013.

19   Kudos Film and Television and ITV, '*Broadchurch* Press Pack', 6 February 2013.

Notes

20 Natalie Clarke, 'The Vicar wears Prada: How the Rev who posed for a fashion shoot in a dog collar has caused a most unholy row among the faithful' *Daily Mail*, 2 December 2012.

21 Christian Research, 'BBC2's *Rev.* – Aunty Beeb subverts stereotypes', April 2014, http://www.christian-research.org/resonate/bbc-s-rev-survey-of-viewers-attitudes/

22 Revd David Robertson, Free Church of Scotland Minister, quoted by Craig Brown, 'Godless TV series *Rev.* shows BBC's bias – minister', *The Scotsman*, 2 May 2014. http://www.scotsman.com/lifestyle/arts/news/godless-tv-series-rev-shows-bbc-s-bias-minister-1-3396404

23 James Mumford, '*Rev.*, the brilliant TV comedy that undermines the church', *Guardian* 28 April 2014 http://www.theguardian.com/commentisfree/2014/apr/28/rev-tv-comedy-undermines-church-of-england

24 Justin Welby, 'Archbishop Justin writes on religious broadcasting in the Radio Times', 16 April 2014 http://www.archbishopofcanterbury.org/articles.php/5300/archbishop-justin-writes-on-religious-broadcasting-in-the-radio-times#sthash.Yp9iUQZ5.dpuf

25 Julia Raeside, 'Have you been watching … *Rev.?*' *Guardian*, 14 April 2014 http://www.theguardian.com/tv-and-radio/tvandradioblog/2014/apr/14/have-you-been-watching-rev

26 James Mumford, '*Rev.*, the brilliant TV comedy that undermines the church' *Guardian* 28 April 2014 http://www.theguardian.com/commentisfree/2014/apr/28/rev-tv-comedy-undermines-church-of-england

27 Jem Bloomfield, 'Rev and Christianity on TV' 28 April 2014, http://quiteirregular.wordpress.com/2014/04/28/rev-and-christianity-on-tv/

28 Stephen Cherry, 'How to Read Rev.' 16 April 2014, http://stephencherry.wordpress.com/2014/04/16/how-to-read-rev/

29 Rowan Williams, 'Faith in the public square', Lecture at Leicester Cathedral, 22 March 2009.

30 Ibid.

31 Stuart Prebble, 'A BBC Trust Review of the Breadth of Opinion Reflected in the BBC's Output', BBC Trust, July 2013.

32 David Hendy, *Life on air: a history of Radio Four*, Oxford, Oxford University Press, 2007.

33 See YouTube video 'Gary and Tracy Richardson's Wedding Flash Mob 15/06/2013' http://www.youtube.com/watch?v=cMrvcORsDLI

The 'bad'

1 Quoted by Alex Epstein, *Crafty TV Writing*, New York, Holt Paperbacks, 2006.

2 Although Michael Gove seemed to think that *Blackadder Goes Forth*, set in the First World War, perpetuated a series of 'myths' about the Great War dreamt up by left-wing academics. *Daily Mail*, 3 January 2014.

3 Piers Morgan Tonight, *CNN*, broadcast 20 January 2011 http://piersmorgan.blogs.cnn.com/2013/09/16/piers-morgan-live-rewind-ricky-gervais-swears-talks-gun-control-crossfire-hosts-on-arming-the-blind-nick-kristof-on-putin/?iref=allsearch

4 BBC One *Are you having a laugh? Comedy and Christianity* directed by Emily Davis, broadcast on Wednesday 27 March 2013.

5 Mayer Nissim and Chris Allen, 'Jimmy Carr on religion: I had an imaginary friend called Jesus – video', *Digital*

Notes

Spy, 25 November 2011 http://www.digitalspy.co.uk/showbiz/news/a351648/jimmy-carr-on-religion-i-had-an-imaginary-friend-called-jesus-video.html

6   Bridget Christie, *The Alternative Comedy Experience*, Comedy Central, Series 1, Episode 3,

7   Dara O Briain, 'Why I don't do Islamic jokes', *Daily Telegraph*, video 1:49PM GMT 23 Nov 2010, http://www.telegraph.co.uk/culture/comedy/8154134/Dara-O-Briain-why-I-dont-do-Islamic-jokes.html.

8   Ben Whitnall, 'Comment: Doing Bible like Eddie Izzard', *The Bible Society,* 3 June 2013, http://www.biblesociety.org.uk/news/comment-doing-bible-like-eddie-izzard/

9   James Martin SJ, *Between Heaven and Mirth*, New York, Harper One, 2011, p. 32f.

10 Ibid, p. 33.

11 BBC One *Are you having a laugh? Comedy and Christianity* directed by Emily Davis, broadcast on Wednesday 27 March 2013.

12 Chapman, Palin, Cleese, *et al., Monty Python's Life of Brian (of Nazareth): Screenplay*, London, Methuen, 2001.

13 BBC One *Are you having a laugh? Comedy and Christianity* directed by Emily Davis, broadcast on Wednesday 27 March 2013.

14 Pope Benedict XVI's phrase – see Greene and Robinson, *Metavista: Bible, Church and Mission in an Age of Imagination,* Milton Keynes, Authentic, 2008, p. 215.

15 Stephen Fry on American versus British Comedy, video https://www.youtube.com/watch?v=8k2AbqTBxao

16 Alexandra Topping 'Olympics opening ceremony: the view from abroad', *Guardian,* Friday 27 July 2012 http://www.theguardian.com/sport/2012/jul/27/olympics-opening-ceremony-view-from-abroad

The 'quirky'

1   Graham Linehan and Arthur Mathews, *Father Ted, the complete scripts*, London, Boxtree, 1999, p. 135.

2   *Small, Far Away – The world of Father Ted*, Hat Trick Productions, 2010.

3   Gerard Gilbert, 'Graham Linehan: I've come to hate the church', *Independent*, 22 June 2013.

4   Graham Linehan and Arthur Mathews, *Father Ted, the complete scripts*, London, Boxtree, 1999, p. 129.

5   Graham Linehan and Arthur Mathews, *Father Ted, the complete scripts*, London, Boxtree, 1999, p. 12.

6   Graham Linehan and Arthur Mathews, *Father Ted, the complete scripts*, London, Boxtree, 1999, p. 8.

7   Graham Linehan and Arthur Mathews, *Father Ted, the complete scripts*, London, Boxtree, 1999, p. 88.

8   Oliver Burkeman, 'Everyone is totally just winging it, all the time", *Guardian*, 21 May 2014 http://www.theguardian.com/news/oliver-burkeman-s-blog/2014/may/21/everyone-is-totally-just-winging-it

9   Graham Linehan and Arthur Mathews, *Father Ted, the complete scripts*, London, Boxtree, 1999, p. 135.

10   Graham Linehan and Arthur Mathews, *Father Ted, the complete scripts*, London, Boxtree, 1999, p. 22.

11   *Small, Far Away – The world of Father Ted*, Hat Trick Productions, 2010.

12   In the original film *Speed*, Keanu Reeves finds himself on a bus which is rigged with a bomb that will detonate if the speed of the van goes below 50 miles per hour. *Speed 2*, widely panned at the time, took the same premise and applied it to a cruise liner.

13   Graham Linehan and Arthur Mathews, *Father Ted, the complete scripts*, London, Boxtree, 1999, p. 295.

Notes

14 Graham Linehan and Arthur Mathews, *Father Ted, the complete scripts*, London, Boxtree, 1999, p. 106.

15 Graham Linehan and Arthur Mathews, *Father Ted, the complete scripts*, London, Boxtree, 1999, p. 45.

16 Gerard Gilbert, 'Graham Linehan: I've come to hate the church', *Independent,* 22 June 2013.

17 Tom Doran, 'Father Ted: comedy as liberation', *Daily Beast,* 3 August 2013.

18 Quoted in Mark I. Pinsky, *The Gospel According to The Simpsons*, Louisville, Westminster John Knox Press, 2001.

19 Jonathan Wynne-Jones, 'Church calls on Fr Homer to reach teenagers', *Daily Telegraph,* 24 June 2007.

20 John Yorke, '*EastEnders*: Faith, Morality and Hope in the Community', speech, 4 September 2002. http://www.bbc.co.uk/pressoffice/speeches/stories/yorke_stalbans.shtml

21 Kerry Harden, '*EastEnders* star June Brown reveals she has changed Dot Branning's scripted lines to fit her personal faith', *Daily Mirror,* 22 June 2014.

22 'EastEnders', BBC, 13 February 2015.

23 Riazatt Butt, 'BBC1 boss: *EastEnders'* Dot is an example of an ordinary Christian on TV', *Guardian*, 14 June 2011.

24 Riazatt Butt, 'BBC1 boss: *EastEnders*' Dot is an example of an ordinary Christian on TV', *Guardian*, 14 June 2011.

25 Ruth Gledhill, 'Church of England congregations fall again, and half are pensioners', *The Times*, 23 January 2010.

26 Kate Fox, *Watching the English*, London, Hodder & Stoughton, 2004, p. 357.

27 Kate Fox, *Watching the English*, London, Hodder & Stoughton, 2004, p. 359.

28 'Big Trouble in Little Wallop' – Making-of Featurette: *Keeping Mum*, Velocity/Think Film, DVD, 2007.

29 'Big Trouble in Little Wallop' – Making-of Featurette: *Keeping Mum*, Velocity/Think Film, DVD, 2007.

30 'Big Trouble in Little Wallop' – Making-of Featurette: *Keeping Mum*, Velocity/Think Film, DVD, 2007.

31 'Big Trouble in Little Wallop' – Making-of Featurette: *Keeping Mum*, Velocity/Think Film, DVD, 2007.

32 Rowan Atkinson, 'The New Archbishop', sketch for Comic Relief, BBC, 2013.

33 'Comic Relief Archbishop sketch draws 2,200 complaints', BBC News, 19 March 2013, http://www.bbc.co.uk/news/entertainment-arts-21846036

34 Ginny Dougary, 'Rowan Atkinson: I cry too much and I find it strange', *The Times*, 24 September 2011.

35 Greene, C. and Robinson, M., *Metavista: Bible, Church and Mission in an Age of Imagination*, Milton Keynes, Authentic, 2008, p. 214.

What would Jesus watch?

1 Kate Fox, *Watching the English,* London, Hodder & Stoughton, 2004, p. 61.

2 James Martin SJ, *Between Heaven and Mirth*, New York, Harper One, 2011, p. 33.

3 James Martin SJ, *Between Heaven and Mirth*, New York, Harper One, 2011, p. 33

Epilogue

1 James Martin SJ, *Between Heaven and Mirth*, New York, Harper One, 2011, p. 70.

2 Emo Philips, 'The Best God Joke Ever, and it's mine!' *Guardian*, 29 September 2005 http://www.theguardian.

Notes

com/stage/2005/sep/29/comedy.religion.

3   James Martin SJ, *Between Heaven and Mirth*, New York, Harper One, 2011, p. 70.

4   Premier Christian Radio, 'Coronation Street to introduce gay vicar', 24 September 2014.